St. John Hankin

St. John Hankin

Edwardian Mephistopheles

William H. Phillips

Rutherford · Madison · Teaneck
Fairleigh Dickinson University Press
London: Associated University Presses

Associated University Presses, Inc.
Cranbury, New Jersey 08512

Associated University Presses
Magdalen House
136–148 Tooley Street
London SE1 2TT, England

Phillips, William H 1940-
   St. John Hankin, Edwardian Mephistopheles.

Bibliography: p.
Includes index.
1. Hankin, St. John Emile Clavering, 1869-1909 –
Criticism and interpretation.
PR6015.A47Z83   822′9′12   77-89783
ISBN 0-8386-2155-4

J6864/5/2

For wife and son,
Eva and Rey:
They helped too

Contents

List of Illustrations

Preface

Before his suicide by drowning in 1909 at the age of 39, St. John Hankin wrote drama reviews for *The Times*, critical essays, prose and verse parodies for *Punch*, short stories, a manuscript of a novel, three one-act plays (the first one he co-authored with Nora Vynne), and five full-length plays, which were all staged in London during his lifetime. After his death Hankin was praised in the press by his good friend George Bernard Shaw, "St. John Hankin's death is a public calamity. He was a most gifted writer of the high comedy of the kind that is a stirring and important criticism of life." Since the 1923 reprinting of Hankin's plays in London and New York, however, his dramatic works have been neglected in both theater and den. *St. John Hankin: Edwardian Mephistopheles* pursues a close reading of Hankin's plays—concentrating as Hankin does on characterizations and themes—and relates Hankin's plays to his parodies and critical essays and to various Victorian and Edwardian plays, especially Shaw's. Hankin's best plays, which depict commonsensical protagonists clashing with upholders of traditional behavior and conventions, are distinctive, lucid, perceptive, and entertaining; three of them could be successfully revived for the stage.

Acknowledgments

With his typical enthusiasm and insight, Harry M. Geduld introduced me to Hankin's plays in 1970.

Samuel Hynes, Stanley Weintraub, and Gerald Weales pointed out major limitations of an early version of the manuscript and thus helped me greatly improve it. Jane W. Stedman's detailed suggestions and questions about a later version of the manuscript were especially constructive. How fortunate for me that I met her at the Enthoven Collection of the Victoria and Albert Museum in the summer of 1974. Robert L. Carringer and L. D. Berkoben read recent versions of the manuscript and made useful stylistic suggestions.

On several different occasions Dan H. Laurence has taken time from his busy schedule to answer in detail my letters of inquiry; some years ago Oscar G. Brockett reassured me about the section on background materials. To both scholars I am grateful.

Mrs. M. L. Hill, Publicity Secretary, Birmingham Repertory Theatre; Anthony Tuckey, Liverpool Playhouse; Susan Hayes, Assistant, Arts Library, The Manchester Public Libraries; Peter Brigg of the University of Guelph, Ontario; and Patricia Reynolds, La Trobe Librarian for the State Library of Victoria, Melbourne all supplied information about productions of Hankin's plays. Miss E. D. Yeo, Assistant Keeper at the Department of Manuscripts at the National Library of Scotland in Edinburgh, sent me copies of three early Hankin letters.

In London, the British Library (formerly the British Museum Library)—including the Reading Room, North Library, the Manuscript Room, and the Colindale Newspaper Library—were invaluable. Also consulted were the Enthoven Collection at the Victoria and Albert Museum, the National Register of Archives, the General Register Office at Somerset House and at St. Catherine House, the British Theatre Museum and Society for Theatre Research Collections at the University of London Library, the Companies Registration House, Guildhall Library, and the Public Record Office. Gordon Phillips, archivist for *The Times*, and Mrs. Constance Kyrle Fletcher, a manuscript dealer were both cooperative and generous with their time.

The library staffs at Indiana University, the New York Public Library, the University of Illinois Library—especially N. Frederick Nash and Mrs. Mary S. Ceibert—the University of California, Berkeley, and especially my home base of California State College, Stanislaus have all helped. Joyce Canty, our department's skillful secretary, typed the penultimate and final drafts.

My helpmate, Eva Santos Phillips, has read all of Hankin's plays, chuckled appreciatively as she did so, and reacted to each of my chapters with perceptive questions and observations. She has also helped in proofreading and has been patient with my demanding, sometimes eccentric, work habits.

As editors, Susan Stock Means and Ronald B. Roth guided me through the interesting final stages of my first book.

August 1978   W. H. P.

St. John Hankin

Mr. St. John Hankin, the Mephistopheles of the new comedy, would have been suspected by an old-fashioned manager—and suspected very justly—of laughing at him.
—Bernard Shaw addressing the guests at the testimonial dinner honoring J. E. Vedrenne and Granville Barker on July 7, 1907

If we are going to discuss ethical questions we must begin by giving the devil fair play. . . . England never does. We always assume that the devil is guilty: and we wont allow him to prove his innocence, because it would be against public morals if he succeeded. . . . And the consequence is that we overreach ourselves; and the devil gets the better of us after all. Perhaps thats what most of us intended him to do.
—Bernard Shaw, *Getting Married*

1
Backdrops:
The Edwardian Period, Its Drama,
Hankin's Life, Some
Apprenticeship Writings

A period of increased striking, class conflict, women's growing
unrest with their lot, continued widespread poverty, alarm over
a falling birthrate, a general belief in the decline of the national
character, a growing doubt in the efficacy of rationalism and
science to solve social problems, a fear of foreign invasion, and
disillusionment over a foreign war—such a period one might
hesitate to designate as "golden." Yet that has been a frequent tag
for the Edwardian era, which began in 1901 with the death of
Queen Victoria and the inauguration of King Edward VII and
concluded with Edward's death in 1910 (or with the beginning
of World War I in 1914—the age is variously delineated). The
growing use of a number of inventions—electric lighting, motor
cars, subways, airplanes, and radiotelegraphy—might suggest
an improvement in the quality of life for Edwardians. And for
the coterie of wealthy, titled, and powerful it was a time of lib-
eration from Victorian restraints. But for many, many more—
such as the servants, the unemployed, the factory workers—life
remained as difficult as under Victoria.

   Intellectually and artistically, the period exhibited a mixture
of the Victorian and the modern. A comparison of the begin-

ning and the ending of the Edwardian era gives some sense of the changes that took place within it. In England the late nineteenth century included

> the years of the Vizetelly [English publisher of Zola's novels, prosecuted in 1888] and Wilde trials, of the ascendancy of the Royal Academy and academic painting, and of the National Vigilance Association. In the last decade of Victoria's reign one could not buy a translation of Zola's *La Terre*, or Dostoevsky's *The Idiot* or *The Possessed* or *The Brothers Karamazov* in London, or see a public performance of Ibsen's *Ghosts*, or look at any picture by a French Impressionist in any gallery, either public or private.[1]

By the beginning of World War I in 1914, however, much now considered modern had evolved. For example, during the Edwardian period Havelock Ellis and Edward Carpenter did research into and published reports about human sexual psychology and behavior. Furthermore, "psychoanalysis, Post-Impressionism, motion picture palaces . . . were all Edwardian additions to the English scene. The first books of Ezra Pound, D. H. Lawrence, James Joyce, and Viginia Woolf and all but one of E. M. Forster's novels are Edwardian; so are the early poems of Eliot, the first sculptures of Epstein and Rutherford's Nobel Prize work in radiation."[2] During the Edwardian years, paintings by Picasso, Cezanne, and Van Gogh were seen in London for the first time, and although Elgar reigned as laureate in the concert halls, the music of Stravinsky, Richard Strauss, and Arnold Schoenberg was heard in England for the first time. In the face of such events numerous conservative organizations, and, as always, individual inertia slowed acceptance of new ideas, new inventions, and new art.

In these changing times the Edwardian theater played a more prominent role in the lives of the Edwardians than we from a vantage point later in the century might assume. Of the Edwardian theater one critic who lived during the era has written:

At no period in history was the theatre ever more popular in this country. All classes of society enjoyed it; it really was the people's pastime. Except for the music-hall it had hardly a rival. Organised sport was then far less developed, motoring was in its infancy and certainly offered no lure except to the rich; there were no dog tracks to entice away the multitude and, of course, the cinema was unknown. True, the public had heard of the "animated pictures" or the "biograph" but only as a curious pendant to music-hall programmes. No one saw in these flickering and fleeting shadows on the screen, in these jerky and scratchy snatches of topical events the germ of what, within a few years, was to be a dangerous rival to the living theatre.

So for the evening entertainment it was either the theatre, the music-hall or the concert, and I am not sure that in the larger areas it was not the theatre that came first when the choice was made.[3]

Within these theaters the age's diverse and changing characteristics were reflected in the variety of fare, including the verse dramas of Stephen Phillips; frequent revivals of abbreviated versions of Shakespeare by actor-manager Henry Irving, then Beerbohm Tree; problem plays populated with titled characters whose values were eventually reaffirmed; farces; melodramas with near-realistic backdrops; the immensely popular musical comedies composed of tuneful songs, comedians, and attractive, scantily-clad, young ladies; revivals; and adaptations, especially from novels.

A minority of critics and playwrights, however, believed that London's theatrical offerings were inadequate: the actor-manager system, long runs, and lack of originality and experimentation were all cited as detrimental. These exponents of the "new drama" championed plays by Shaw, Galsworthy, Granville Barker, Hankin, and various contemporary European playwrights. Such plays tended to question commonplace assumptions and to treat their subjects more thoroughly and more consistently than did

the staple West End products, including those of Jones and
Pinero.

This greater willingness by some dramatists to deal with serious topics in a more uncompromising way exacerbated the
friction between playwrights, on the one hand, and the censor
and the managers (and often critics), on the other. Consequently,
from the 1890s on, questions about the role of the Lord Chamberlain's Office, which censored plays in London from 1737 to 1968,
were raised frequently and urgently, particularly by avant-garde
playwrights.

> Between 1895 and 1909, out of some eight thousand plays
> submitted to the Chamberlain only thirty were banned. But
> these included works by some of the leading writers of the
> age. Another thirteen or fourteen were banned temporarily,
> because the authors refused to "modify" their work as the
> censor suggested, but licences were later granted. Many more
> plays were altered in pettifogging detail, at the censor's re-
> quest, for apparently ludicrous reasons. Nobody knows how
> many were left unwritten because, as the Lord Chamber-
> lain said in 1866, authors "know pretty well what will be
> allowed." And there is no figure for the plays which *were* writ-
> ten but never submitted to the Chamberlain, because he
> suggested, in anticipation, that it would be a waste of time.
> Yet it should not be forgotten that the censor did not pursue
> any systematic, ruthless interference with the theatre. He
> passed dozens of plays that he *might* have vetoed, judging by
> the standards he applied to those he *did* ban. It was in fact the
> unpredictable, inconsistent, arbitrary character of the censor-
> ship which did so much to inflame its enemies.[4]

In the last decade of the nineteenth century and in the first
decade of the twentieth, the Lord Chamberlain seemed most
censorious of such matters as premarital sex, adultery, venereal
disease, abortion, and prostitution.

To avoid the Lord Chamberlain's censorship and to encourage
original dramas, numerous London theater groups were formed.
Of the theatrical societies and clubs founded after the birth of

J. T. Grein's Independent Theatre in 1891, The New Century Theatre, founded by William Archer in 1897; The Pioneers, founded in 1905; The Literary Theatre Society, founded in 1906; and The Play Actors' Society, founded in 1907 were among the most important, but their contributions to the advancement of the new drama were overshadowed by those of the Stage Society and the Court Theatre.

In the years following the demise of the Independent Theatre, its ideals were perpetuated and its goals more fully attained by the Stage Society. The chairman of the Producing Committee during its first season was Bernard Shaw himself. Initially, the Society agreed *"to meet once a month and to give at least six performances throughout the year in large studios on Sunday evenings. The plays were to be without scenery in draped backgrounds, and to include 'high comedy' as well as more serious works, English as well as continental."*[5] The Stage Society never had a theater of its own; instead, it rented available theaters and halls. By giving Sunday performances—a daring move in late Victorian England—the society could secure professional actors and actresses. From 1899 to 1909 the Stage Society encouraged such new native playwrights as Shaw, Granville Barker, Hankin, Maugham, and Arnold Bennett; staged plays by such major foreign playwrights as Tolstoy, Gorki, Gogol, Brieux, de Curel, Hauptmann, Sudermann, Wedekind, Heijermans, Maeterlinck, and Ibsen; and produced censored plays by Maeterlinck, Brieux, Shaw, Barker, and Edward Garnett.[6] From 1899 to 1909 the society produced sixty-two plays—including the first stagings of Shaw's *Candida, Mrs. Warren's Profession,* and *Man and Superman.*

The Court Theatre of 1904 to 1907—a descendant of the Théâtre Libre, Independent Theatre, and the Stage Society—was another London Theater group that supported plays of literary and artistic merit. But unlike the directors of the Independent Theatre and the Stage Society, the Court Theatre management of J. E. Vedrenne and Granville Barker secured a permanent home in which to present new plays for short runs. As Desmond Mac-Carthy observed, the Court Theatre succeeded and had influence because of its "determination to get away from what was artificial and theatrical in methods and traditions, and to get back to actuality in gesture, diction, and sentiment."[7] From October 1904 to June 1907, the Court Theatre produced thirty-two plays by seventeen authors. (*Don Juan in Hell* and *Man and Superman* are counted as separate plays.) The Court Theatre's foremost achievement was in bringing Shaw to a wide audience. Its first production was *Candida*; eleven of its plays were by Shaw; and 701 out of 988 performances were of Shavian plays.[8] Additionally, the Court Theatre staged plays by Barker, Galsworthy, Hankin, Housman, Yeats, Masefield, Euripides, Hauptmann, Schnitzler, Ibsen, and Maeterlinck, as well as several other dramatists now obscure. Stage Society and Court Theatre plays helped end England's isolation from contemporary European dramas; stimulated the founding of repertory theaters in Manchester, Glasgow, Liverpool, and Birmingham; and encouraged British playwrights who rejected the themes and dramaturgy of both Victorian predecessors and their immediate heirs in the commercial Edwardian theater.

Of this group of emerging dramatists, St. John Hankin, whose five full-length plays were first produced by either the Stage Society or the Court Theatre, played a prominent role.[9]

In June of 1909, St. John Hankin went to the baths at Llandrindod Wells, Wales. There on a "dull, sultry, wet" day after receiving in the mails a portrait of his mother who had died just one month before, he left a note for his wife saying he feared he would "slip into invalidism" (as his father had done), strapped two seven-pound dumbbells around his neck, and jumped into the river Ithon.[10] After an inquest was held, his body was cremated, a funeral service was held, and his ashes placed in an urn at the Golder's Green Cemetery in London.

Unfortunately, few other events in Hankin's life are known in as much detail as his last days. For him there is neither a biography nor a collection of letters. The brief entry in the *Dictionary of National Biography* discloses only the basic facts. His own writings only obliquely reveal any biographical data. It is difficult to trace surviving relatives and get them to reveal (or remember) detailed information about him. Hankin's publishers, too, are of limited help.

So little of Hankin's life is known that the following biography is little more than an outline (see Appendix A). St. John Hankin was born in Southampton on 25 September 1869, the third and youngest son of four children. (Various sources have erroneously listed his birth year as 1870.) His father, Charles Wright Hankin, was at the time of Hankin's birth director of the King Edward VI Grammar School of Southampton; during St. John's lifetime, his father was to suffer a nervous breakdown and become an invalid. Hankin's mother, Mary Louisa Perrot Hankin, who published a small book of verse in 1892, was described by Hankin's widow as "a brilliant woman, also of good family with a distinct literary gift from whom my husband inherited much of his charm and ability both as a conversationalist and as a man of letters." [11]

In 1883 Hankin entered Malvern Public School, Worcester, and at the age of seventeen he matriculated at Merton College, Oxford, where he studied classics for four years. After leaving Oxford in 1890, he got, according to his widow, "several good appointments as private tutor, which enabled him to see a good deal of society." [12]

He began a journalistic career in London also in 1890. Beginning in that year he was a contributor to *The Saturday Review*. Unfortunately, since these articles are unsigned and no record of them has been discovered, his contributions to that distinguished London periodical remain unidentified. He first tried his hand at writing for the stage in 1893, when he co-authored with Nora Vynne a one-act play. *Andrew Paterson*, the result, extols the spontaneity of youth not the prudence of age in matters of the heart. In 1894 he joined the staff of *The Indian Daily News* of Calcutta. Thus far, his writings for that paper are also unidentified. After contracting malaria, Hankin returned to London probably in late 1894. From that time until at least 1899, he evidently lived with his parents in London (see fig. 1.).

From his return to London until his first play was staged in 1903, Hankin's writings include articles, stories, a novel and book reviews. From 1897 to 1899 he also wrote about seventy drama reviews for *The Times*. Hankin's reviews of revivals, adaptations, melodramas, musical comedies, farces, and occasional original serious dramas mirror the London theater of the late 1890s—before Shaw, Barker, and Hankin and before the Stage Society and similar independent theater groups gained influence. Hankin's reviews prove, too, that he had seen and analyzed a variety of plays (see Selected Bibliography). Such experience—particularly since no evidence reveals that Hankin was ever involved in acting or any aspect of staging—gave him insight into what is effective in the theater. From 1898 until his first play was staged in 1903, Hankin also wrote more than one-hundred short satiric pieces for *Punch*[13] including forty-four dramatizations of novels, "last acts" to various plays, and reworkings and compressions of plays already staged. Also targets for his satire were drama critics, actor-managers, various Victorian poets, politicians and political events, military officers, journalists, scholars, mountain climbing, aviation, auto racing, the inefficient London telephone system, polluted London fog, and many other subjects. In 1901 some of his writings from *Punch* were reprinted as *Mr. Punch's Dramatic Sequels*, a series of comic last acts to various famous plays.

In the same year Hankin married Florence Routledge, who was ten years his senior and was the daughter of the publisher George Routledge. The marriage was to be childless and evidently happy. On the wedding certificate Hankin's occupation was listed as "journalist," but shortly after they were married, by Florence Hankin's later account, Hankin devoted most of his time to writing plays. From at least as early as 1902, Hankin took a role in running the Stage Society. For the 1903–1904 season he was "Hon.–Librarian," and from at least as early as 1902 until his death, he served on the Council of Management.

The Two Mr. Wetherbys, Hankin's initial full-length play, was first performed by the Stage Society in February of 1903

Autograph and Photograph of St. John Hankin
in 1897, at age twenty-seven

and received mixed but encouraging reviews. In 1904 was published his *Lost Masterpieces and Other Verses*, a reprinting primarily from *Punch* and *St. James's Gazette* of parodies of famous poets, especially Victorians.[14] Still suffering from poor health, which he attributed to his year's stay in India, he retired in 1905 to Campden, Gloucestershire, where he spent most of his time writing plays. In that same year Brieux's *Les Trois Filles de Monsieur Dupont*, which Hankin had translated, was produced by the Stage Society after the Lord Chamberlain's Office refused to license the play. From 1905 to 1907 three Hankin plays were first staged: *The Return of the Prodigal* (Court Theatre), *The Charity that Began at Home* (Court Theatre), and *The Cassilis Engagement* (Stage Society). Late in 1908, his one-act farce, *The Burglar Who Failed*, was staged; for the first time a Hankin play was in a commercial theater. One month later, the Stage Society produced his final full-length play, *The Last of the De Mullins*.

According to his widow, "about 1907 his attacks of neurasthenie began to come on more frequently and lasted longer so that after 1908 he made little headway with imaginative work."[15] In 1908 he underwent surgery; in the spring of the same year he went to France, perhaps for the sake of his health. Late in the year he made out his will.

Three years after his death, his one-act play *The Constant Lover*, was finally staged, and a three-volume edition of his plays was published in London and New York. At about this time fellow playwright George Calderon finished Hankin's manuscript for *Thompson*, and in 1913 the play had a short run. During the teens and twenties Hankin's plays were popular with audiences in the provinces, especially in Birmingham and Manchester (see Appendix C), and in 1923 Hankin's dramatic works were reprinted in a two-volume edition.

The records give no particularly vivid image of Hankin's personality either. Certainly Hankin was not universally liked in Edwardian London. Partially for personal reasons he was blackballed from the newly formed Dramatists' Club in the spring of 1909. And Hankin's attacks against such established figures as playwright Arthur Wing Pinero caused Hankin some unpopularity. Pinero, for example, wrote to Shaw in 1910, "When he was alive, he used consistently to attack men who were more successful than himself, and that was not considered quite good form—men, I mean, practising the same calling as himself." Even Shaw, who frequently defended Hankin and his drama, described Hankin as conceited.[16]

Most of the accounts of Hankin—by Shaw and others— are much more positive. In an interview Shaw reported, "In his recent letters to me . . . there was nothing that prepared me in the very least for the shock of his death. He complained that he had never been himself since he had undergone some surgical treatment last year, and that he could not write easily; but he touched on all this with his usual gaiety."[17] A few years after Hankin's death, John Drinkwater in his Introduction to Hankin's dramatic works noted, "St. John Hankin was proud of his work, and made frank avowal of the fact. 'You always think so well of your own plays, Hankin,' said a colleague. 'Of course I do,' was the reply, 'otherwise I shouldn't continue to write them.' The statement implies no undue self-satisfaction. He was not easily content with the thing he had written, and was a finely conscientious workman in revision and the search for rightness in balance and form. But the task done, he was glad to stand by it and said so."[18] Arnold Bennett implied that Hankin was a greater conversationalist than Shaw and elsewhere wrote that "beneath the somewhat finicking manner there was visible the intelligence that cared for neither conventions nor traditions, nor for possible inconvenient results, but solely for intellectual honesty amid conditions of intellectual freedom."[19]

More intimate glimpses of Hankin are given by a friend and by his widow. Right after Hankin's death, a drama critic related, "We often held widely opposite views about the drama, and used to argue with the frankness of old friends, while he would send me his plays as they came out with inscriptions such as 'These, though you won't like them, with the author's love.' "[20] Mrs. Hankin reported that her husband "was a personal friend of most of the literary people in London during the 90th [*sic*] and the first decade of the present century. He liked and admired Bernard Shaw who was a good friend to him, also Harley Granville Barker, Galsworthy, and Sir Edmund Gosse."[21] Mrs. Hankin also reported that her husband played golf and tennis for his health and that "he was subject to ups and downs in spirits. He was sensitive and highly strung. He was extremely lively and extremely bright often, but the moment he did not feel quite lively he could not do his work."[22]

One might expect Hankin's personality to emerge from an interview published just two months before his death (reprinted in Appendix B). In the interview, however, Hankin talks not about himself but about his plays. He reveals little of his character except by his ironic tone, occasionally more disturbing than amusing because he seems to mask pain with humor. Speaking of the casting of the original production of *The Return of the Prodigal*, for example, he says, "I shall never get a better cast for a play though I live to be as old as Pinero—which, by the way, I hope not to do!"[23] Hankin concludes the interview on another note more ominous than amusing, "I have a comedy—a very light comedy—struggling to come to birth, and if only I get to Algiers or somewhere where the sun shines, I may be able to write it. Nobody can possibly write a light comedy in a north-east wind, can they? A north-easter killed even Charles Kingsley."[24] To the last, Hankin appears amusing, yet melancholy and elusive.

Hankin's biography is so sketchy that it is of little help in understanding his plays. Of more use are his early writings.

As a journalist from 1890 to 1903, Hankin wrote in numerous genres and about an immense range of subjects (see Selected Bibliography, where many of his writings are briefly described). From this mass of early writings I have selected two essays and a dramatic parody that foreshadow the preoccupations, outlook, and approach of Hankin's later drama.

Two of Hankin's early essays reveal many of the views of his later plays. "The Criminal" (1893) points out the inadequacies of the prison system and suggests medical, mental, and physical therapy for the correctible—death for the incorrigible. The essay, although written when Hankin was only twenty-three, reveals qualities that were to characterize his writings for the rest of his life: both his doubts about reforming human nature and his willingness to follow an argument to wherever it leads him, even if to an unconventional and unpopular position. Like a few of Hankin's later writings, the essay is also tinged with bitterness.

A later essay, "The True Sublime of Boating" (1898), contains both practical advice and enthusiastic opinions about how to drift down English rivers in a canoe and suggests how much Hankin appreciated peaceful country settings: "Thus you will spend your days in green places, far away from the smoke of factories, the clatter of traffic, the restless turmoil of life." The philosophy of relaxation and enjoyment away from the hubbub of commercial late Victorian England was recurrent in his work; it was later espoused and enacted amusingly by such Hankin protagonists as Richard Wetherby (*The Two Mr. Wetherbys*), Eustace Jackson (*The Return of the Prodigal*), Hugh Verreker (*The Charity that Began at Home*), and Cecil Harburton (*The Constant Lover*).

From 1898 to 1903 Hankin wrote forty-four short dramatizations for *Punch* (see Selected Bibliography). Of these, five are of novels; six of types of national and mostly adapted drama; twelve from plays by Sophocles, Euripides, Shakespeare, Sheridan, and Goldsmith; four from Maeterlinck, Ibsen, and Gorki; and seventeen from nineteenth- and early twentieth-century British works.

One of Hankin's last dramatic parodies is an embryonic Hankin play. Only five months before the Stage Society produced his *The Two Mr. Wetherbys*, Hankin parodied Henry Arthur Jones's *Chance, the Idol*. In Jones's play, Ellen Farndon, a bank clerk's daughter, had been seduced by the aristocratic Alan Leversage and had had a son by him. Now at Monte Carlo she tries to use 2,000 pounds to win him by paying off his debts and gaining a small fortune. The amount, however, is deemed insufficient, so she tries the roulette table. At first, chance favors her, and she pays off his debts. Then she loses her remaining money. Her lover, who has been bullied by his snobbish Aunt Mary, turns to a wealthy girl of his own class, and Ellen resolves to begin a new life with her son and leaves.

In Hankin's version, "Chance and the Idle," all reference to the fatherless child is omitted. Alan has promised to marry Ellen and would prefer to do so, but his aunt, Lady Mary Nobody, insists that he marry a rich lady. When Ellen arrives, Aunt Mary demands she forget about marrying Alan. Ellen then discloses that she has some money, but the aunt says 2,000 pounds is insufficient. Ellen gambles and turns the amount into 8,000 pounds. The aunt agrees that the amount is enough for an engagement—but not a marriage. Ellen tries her luck once more, loses all her money, and is rejected by Lady Mary and her nephew.

In his parody Hankin satirizes the upper class for its nonproductivity (Alan refuses to work) and for its practice of marrying off impoverished young men with a name or position to rich ladies (Alan, we learn, is a bargain-priced "Slopshire Nobody"). As he was to do in his plays, Hankin also satirizes both the imposing, aristocratic ladylike character and the young people willing to follow conventional dictates. In fact, as in Hankin's second play, *The Return of the Prodigal*, the impoverished aristocrats—not the impulsive, poor, young protagonist—are the more ridiculed. Hankin's later drama suggests that he might agree with the sympathies of Jones's play, but in dealing with such themes Hankin would take a lighter yet more satiric approach.

In *Punch* Hankin parodied plays by dramatists he admired, such as Shakespeare, Ibsen, and Shaw, as well as those by more commercial playwrights he scarcely revered, such as A. W. Pinero and Hall Caine. As plays to parody Hankin chose both critically acclaimed and popular narratives and applied his logic; the results are often amusing, genial, and surprising. Frequently as in his parodies of Robertson's *Caste* and Pinero's *The Second*

Mrs. Tanqueray, he extended an ending and showed a likely fate for the characters. In their unconventional yet consistent endings, surprising characters, and pointed satire, Hankin's forty-four short dramatizations for *Punch* are significant forerunners of his plays. In these early playlets—all but one of which was published before Hankin's first play was staged—Hankin practiced his craft on a modest scale while often displaying dissatisfaction with the commercial London stage.

Hankin's publications as a journalist reveal his versatility and skill. Occasionally, these early writings help in understanding his plays; thus, further reference will be made to them. During his apprenticeship Hankin wrote in many genres and about a vast range of subjects, including political, military, economic, and social issues largely untouched upon by his later plays. Even from his earliest writings about conventional behavior and accepted beliefs, the "Edwardian Mephistopheles" displayed amusing, commonsensical, judicious criticism but also occasional bitter outbursts. His early writings show a preference and talent for parody, satire, and drama. These experiences and preoccupations led Hankin in his remaining years to devote himself to writing for the stage.

Notes

1. Samuel Hynes, *The Edwardian Turn of Mind* (Princeton: Princeton University Press, 1968), pp. 307-8.

2. Ibid., p. 5.

3. A. E. Wilson, *Edwardian Theatre* (London: Arthur Barker, 1951), pp. 22-23.

4. Richard Findlater, *Banned! A Review of Theatrical Censorship in Britian* (London: Mac-Gibbon & Kee, 1967), p. 79. For further information on theatrical censorship in England, see the studies cited in the bibliography of Findlater's book, pp. 225-26.

5. C. B. Purdom, "Commentary," in *Bernard Shaw's Letters to Granville Barker*, ed. Purdom (New York: Theatre Art Books, 1957), p. 3.

6. Foreword to *The Incorporated Stage Society: Ten Years, 1899 to 1909* (London: Chiswick Press, 1909), pp. 7-9.

7. Desmond MacCarthy, *The Court Theatre 1904-1907*, ed. Stanley Weintraub (1907; reprint ed., Coral Gables, Fla.: University of Miami Press, 1966), pp. 11-12.

8. Ibid., p. 107.

9. For an overview of the plays produced by the Stage Society from 1899 to 1909 and by the Court Theatre from 1904 to 1907, see *The Incorporated Stage Society* and *The Court Theatre 1904-1907*. An indispensable reference work in studying Edwardian theater-and all English drama up to 1909-is *"The Stage" Cyclopaedia: A Bibliography of Plays*, compiled by H. J. Eldredge (London: "The Stage," 1909). It lists title, author, genre, source, number of acts, and theater and opening date of major productions.

10. *Radnor Express*, 24 June 1909, p. 3.

11. Quoted in Gertrud Engel, *St. John Hankin als Dramatiker* (PhD. diss., University of Giessen, 1931) (Giessen: Buchdruckerei Nitschkowski, 1931), p. 11.

12. Quoted in ibid., p. 11.

13. Sister de Chantal Whelan, "St. John Hankin's Dramatic Esthetic: Its Theory and Practice" (PhD. Diss., Indiana University 1973).

14. The *St. Jame's Gazette*, which became the *Evening Standard*, has no records as old as 1909, so it is difficult to determine if Hankin wrote material for that newspaper not included in *Lost Masterpieces*.

15. Quoted in Engel, *St. John Hankin*, p. 11.

16. Arthur W. Pinero, "To G. B. Shaw," in *The Collected Letters of Arthur W. Pinero*, ed. J. P. Wearing (Minneapolis, Minn.: University of Minnesota Press, 1974), p. 226 and Bernard Shaw, "To Arthur W. Pinero," in *Collected Letters 1898-1910*, ed. Dan H. Laurence (New York: Dodd, Mead, 1972), p. 912.

17. *Daily News*, 21 June 1909, p. 7.

18. John Drinkwater, Introduction to *The Dramatic Works of St. John Hankin*, ed. Drinkwater (London: Martin Secker, 1912), 1: 3.

19. *Journals*, ed. Newman Flower (London: Cassell, 1932), pp. 276-77, and *Books and Persons* (London: Chatto & Windus, 1917), p. 142.

20. *Truth* 65 (23 June 1909): 1508.

21. Quoted in Engel, *St. John Hankin*, p. 12.

22. *Radnor Express*, p. 3.

23. "In the Days of my Youth," *M.A.P.* 22 (10 April 1909): 348.

24. Ibid., p. 349.

2
"A Middle-Class Comedy":
The Two Mr. Wetherbys

> Every artist begins by imitating some one.
> Even the greatest genius does not spring full–
> born from the head of Zeus. After a time he
> "finds himself," and ceases to be an echo, but in
> the beginning he models himself on others.[1]

So wrote St. John Hankin in 1908 about Oscar Wilde. But this quotation applies as well to Hankin. Although *The Two Mr. Wetherbys* (Stage Society, March 1903) embodies the satiric outlook of Hankin's earlier works in its sensible and often amusing protagonist, the play sometimes works at cross purposes and is highly derivative.

The play, subtitled *A Middle-Class Comedy*, is set in a suburban home having only one servant, and its protagonist is in an unnamed business with his brother. The sisters Margaret and Constantia are married to the brothers James and Richard, known respectively as the good and the bad Mr. Wetherby. The other significant characters are Robert Carne, and Clara, who is aunt to Margaret, Constantia, and Robert. James is saddled with Clara and Robert, both of whom preach duty and principles to him. James's cheerful brother, Richard, has been separated from his wife 'for a year. Under the terms of the separation, Richard and Constantia are to meet once a year to see

if a reconciliation is possible. Early in the play we learn that
their meeting, to take place at James's house, is imminent. Robert
and Aunt Clara both counsel Constantia to be unforgiving,
but Constantia chafes at the inconveniences of separation and
wants a reconciliation; she says that she intends to accept Richard
back after he repents. In their meeting, however, the insouciant
Richard says that, since she wants to return only out of duty,
he refuses to take her back.

The second act opens with James, Clara, and Richard at
dinner where Richard displays his appetite and levity. After
Clara leaves in a huff, we learn that James, under the pretext
of attending missionary meetings, often goes out with Richard
for card playing and music halls. The two discuss their different ways of life: Richard advocates his honest approach, whereas James admits to the strain and fatigue of his hypocritical
ways. Richard's spirits finally cheer James, and they decide
to go to a music hall.

In the second scene of the second act Margaret takes James's
coat offstage, where she finds a music-hall program in it. Encouraged by Richard, James confesses that he has been leading
a dual life and asks forgiveness. Margaret, however, vows to
leave him.

In the last act Margaret is still resolved to leave and asks
Constantia if she may stay with her, but Constantia says she
must control Richard's corrupting influence by going back
to live with him. Richard again refuses to take her back and
plans to share his apartment with James. But Richard sees that
James and Margaret love each other, so he shrewdly tells Margaret
that if she tries to get James back he will become like Richard
and reject her. Margaret sees her error and is reconciled to her
husband. James then vows not to go out with Richard again,
but Margaret now argues in Richard's favor, insisting only
that henceforth James hide nothing from her. Margaret also
declares that Clara and Robert must leave. James and Margaret
then encourage Richard to accept Constantia, and he succumbs
to a reconciliation. "*At second curtain* CONSTANTIA *is by door,*

followed by DICK *carrying Both . . .* [his and Constantia's] *bags."*

Aunt Clara and Robert, on the one hand, and Richard Wetherby, on the other, are the play's antagonists. Clara is the first
of many Hankin characters rigidly against change. She is the
voice of duty, or the conventional behavior dictated by the old,
the parental, and the conservative. At her last appearance, about
halfway through the play, she is so upset by Richard's high
spirits that she leaves the dinner table, proclaiming, "I cannot
be a witness to any more of this levity."[2] A descendant of Oscar
Wilde's Lady Markby of *An Ideal Husband* and Lady Bracknell
and Miss Prism of *The Importance of Being Earnest*, Clara, a stock
character, represents duty, status quo, and joylessness.

Clara's nephew, Robert, lives to visit her, to give advice, and
to collect subscriptions for various causes. The Otaheite [Ta-
hiti] mission, Mahommedan Conversion Fund, Married Woman's Protection League, Bishop's Sustentation Fund, Tobago
Diocesan Conference, Hairy Ainos Protection Society, and Nova
Zembla Mission are among the movements Robert champions.
Hankin satirizes the abundance, specialization, and impracticality
of such causes, perhaps since he thought man unreformable.
The antithesis to the robust, cheerful Richard, Robert dodders
around and takes "gentle" walks. He is *"a cadaverous shambling
man," "a solemn prig with no digestion,"* and a victim of insomnia.
When he is not being "unctuous," he moons or sulks. Once,
when Margaret and James hug, Robert *"stands by the window
gloomily observing the embrace, then turns away."* A character type
like Clara, he is the butt of jokes, but lifeless, and an ineffectual
adversary for Richard.

Initially, Margaret is completely under Clara's and Robert's
sway. She believes so firmly in Clara and Robert that she nearly
leaves her husband when she discovers his rather harmless decep-
tion. But by the end of the play Richard has educated her; she
both banishes Clara and Robert and forgives James his hypocrisy
when he promises to be honest from then on.

Constantia also finds it difficult to live by the Clara/Robert
ideals: she is influenced by both the code of expected conduct

and her own wants. Consequently, like characters from Shaw's earlier plays,[3] she sometimes uses "duty" to disguise her self-interests. She calls it her painful duty to accept back her husband, but because of the inconveniences that she faces as a separated wife, *she* wants him back:

> CONSTANTIA. No. I shall not forgive him. He has not deserved that. But I shall go back to him. I cannot allow him to retain his liberty any longer. When I separated from him it was to punish his misconduct and give him an opportunity for repentance, not to enable him to plunge deeper into vice and folly. [*Crosses to Fire*]
> MARGARET. But Constantia! *Ought* you to do this? Won't you be very unhappy? [*Rises.*]
> CONSTANTIA [*calmly*] : I shall be able to bear it. Indeed, I have not found my life apart from Richard so happy either. The house is very small and the dining-room chimney smokes. [*Sits at desk.*] Of course these things do not *weigh* with me, but they exist. And you must remember that it was *duty* which made me leave my husband, not pleasure.

At first Constantia tries to win her husband back while upholding the duty that Clara and Robert preach. But as the play progresses, she becomes increasingly desperate. Finally, she tacitly asks Richard for forgiveness and presumably repudiates her belief that marriage entails duty for the wife and reformation for the husband.

James seems to do what is expected of him, but the play reveals his misery. Early in his marriage James had been willing to try to act as Margaret, Robert, and Clara expect. Soon, however, he had abandoned his austere behavior: "And after a time—six months or so—I found I couldn't keep it up. I wanted amusement. But by that time I was saddled with my ghastly reputation. And I've been groaning under it ever since." Surprisingly, as the play implies on several occasions, a good reputation—not a bad one—is a burden to its owner. Until Richard's intervention,

Clara and Robert bore James, hamper his affection for his wife, and in general make his life a trial in his own home.

Into this oppressive atmosphere enters Richard. He is a fully developed character, and most critics have praised him highly. An exception was A. B. Walkley, the influential critic for *The Times*, who displayed his typical Victorian propriety by chiding Hankin that "a little more pains might have been taken to show that the uxorious James, despite all his pusillanimity, is after all a far better fellow than his brother."[4] Closer to the mark is a more recent opinion: "Richard Wetherby is pure Hankin, the type of intelligent and charming egoist whose 'system' consists in confronting pretense with honesty, romantic nonsense with cynical common sense, self-deceit with self-awareness. He infuriates the solemn and the dedicated types who have lost all relish for life's pleasures and disturbs the conventionalists by his lack of concern for reputation and common opinion."[5]

Richard's philosophy is summed up: "I sleep well, eat well—you don't, Jim—I make no pretence of being better than I am. Rather the contrary. And I find the world a very pleasant, amusing place." Only Richard appreciates beautiful weather, sleeps soundly, and, like Algernon in Wilde's *The Importance of Being Earnest*, he could agree with the sentiments of the gourmet narrator in the last two stanzas of Hankin's poem in *Punch*, "Ode to Spring";

> Thy [Spring's] lark that soaring high
> Her liquid strain
> Again and yet again
> Pours forth in ecstasy
> Maketh an even more ecstatic pie
> Thy little lambs
> That frisk and bleat
> Beside their dams
> Are excellent to eat
> While in thy limpid streamlets lurks the trout
> (I like him even better *out*!)

Therefore, Sweet Spring, thy name
Ever will I acclaim,
And while thy food
Remaineth good
I will exalt the same

Joking, Richard says, also keeps him healthy. And Richard is proof that it is best to be oneself and to be truthful. Like such Shavian heroes as Andrew Undershaft and Napoleon and like Lord Goring of Wilde's *An Ideal Husband*, Richard is avowedly selfish: "No, I'm not [an altruist]. But I've got a good temper and a rattling good digestion. That's enough for *me*." In contrast to the other male character of five-and-thirty—the shambling, cadaverous Robert—Richard is "*a handsome, careless, jovial-looking man . . . very cheerful and quite at his ease*," and he speaks directly, simply, and energetically.

As the epigraph to the play, Hankin quotes Horace Walpole: "*Life is a comedy to those who think, a tragedy to those who feel*." Richard acts as if it is better to see life—in spite of its vicissitudes—as a comedy. When Margaret follows Constantia's example and plans to leave James, he looks "*unutterably depressed*," whereas Dick responds, "Curious how much alike sisters are. . . . I remember an almost similar scene a year ago with Constantia. The marriage tie seems to sit loosely on our family." Although Richard is largely unmoved, he is not simply an aloof rationalist. For example, he saves James and Margaret's marriage, and he can be a sympathetic listener. By disrupting the stultifying environment of the play and by helping make possible both the routing of Aunt Clara and Robert and the reconciliation of James and Margaret on more honest terms, he wins our sympathy and enriches the play with its commonsensical views.

Unfortunately, the themes that are carefully developed throughout the play's first two acts are undercut by the implausible character transformations in the last act. Within a matter of minutes, Margaret decides to leave James and live with Constantia; Constantia resolves to return to Richard; Richard decides to live with James; Richard reconciles James and Margaret; Margaret decides to expel Robert and Clara; James criticizes Richard while Margaret now defends him; and James and Margaret reconcile Richard and Constantia. Although amusing, this action reveals two glaring inconsistencies in characterization: Margaret's sudden willingness to expel Robert and Clara and Richard's startling decision to return to the married yoke. Act 1 concludes with Richard's rejecting Constantia's excuses for the inconveniences she faces as a separated wife. Contrarily, the last act ends with Richard's making only these conditions for accepting Constantia back: "Look here, Con, if you'll say you're sorry for the way you've treated me, and will let me do everything that I please in future and always laugh at my jokes, I'll forgive you." No mention is made of love, affection, and tastes, no mention of the folly of adhering to duty, for all of which Richard had argued so amusingly yet persuasively.

In many of Hankin's early dramatic sequels and in a later essay he criticized improbable endings and dramatic critics who judge a play only as "the plot of a comedy," not "as a piece of real life," and to whom "all engagements are satisfactory and all marriages are made in Heaven, and at the mere thought of wedding bells they dodder like romantic old women in an almshouse."[6] It is curious that in his first play Hankin wrote an enervating conclusion. In *The Two Mr. Wetherbys* Hankin yielded to the temptation of an amusing, farcical conclusion of the kind often found in his short dramatizations in *Punch*. Hankin's first play sometimes reveals characters in fresh detail, but much of the material is well worn, and Hankin does not particularly seem to aim to present "a piece of real life." Thus, Richard and his commonsense ideas are abandoned for an improbable, farcical ending—satisfying to audiences bred on "happy endings" but at variance with the play's characters and themes.

In his first play, Hankin was not yet his own man. Of all Hankin's plays *The Two Mr. Wetherbys* shows the strongest marks of Oscar Wilde. In its wit, its character types (especially the dominating old woman), and its characters' role playing to avoid boredom, *The Two Mr. Wetherbys* echoes *The Importance of Being Earnest.*

The Two Mr. Wetherbys has even clearer similarities to *An Ideal Husband* (1895).[7] Wilde's play is often melodramatic, has a complicated plot, and displays much wit merely for wit's sake, yet the main characters and situation of *The Two Mr. Wetherbys* are remarkably close to those of *An Ideal Husband.* Like Richard Wetherby, Lord Goring is in his mid-thirties and is an easy going, disreputable hedonist. But, also like Richard, Lord Goring can be kind, serious, and constructive, as when his good friend Sir Robert Chiltern needs help in dealing with the machinations of Mrs. Cheveley. Sir Robert is a kind of "good" Mr. Wetherby: his career and reputation are not what they seem. Sir Robert's wife, like Margaret Wetherby, thinks him an "ideal husband," and she is disillusioned, then reconciled to him by play's end. Both *An Ideal Husband* and *The Two Mr. Wetherbys* are partly about the hypocrisy encouraged by the widespread demands in Victorian England for moral purity by fallible people.

Hankin's first play also has affinities to *The Serious Family*[8] — Morris Barnett's mid-nineteenth-century free adaptation of J. F. A. Bayard's *Le Mari à la Campagne ou Le Tartuffe moderne.* The similarities in plot and characterization between *The Serious Family* and *The Two Mr. Wetherbys* are too numerous to be coincidental. Like *The Serious Family, The Two Mr. Wetherbys* shows a candid and unconventional visitor precipitating a crisis in the home of his similarly inclined but hypocritical brother/ friend. In both plays the visitor eventually works a reconciliation between husband and wife and helps rout the two puritanical characters who had encouraged the husband's unhappy dual life.

Although Richard Wetherby derives from plays by Shaw and, more so, Wilde's plays and dramas like *The Serious Family*, he is a vital and provocative creation. As a debut *The Two Mr. Wetherbys* is impressive and amusing, but derivative and limited. In sacrificing character to plot, *The Two Mr. Wetherbys* is false to its themes and marred as serious comedy. Happily, in most later Hankin plays greater originality and consistency in characterization and theme prevail.

Notes

1. St. John Hankin, "The Collected Plays of Oscar Wilde," in *The Dramatic Works of St. John Hankin*, ed. John Drinkwater (London: Martin Secker, 1912), 3: 185. This essay, which is still a useful assessment of Wilde's drama, displays Hankin's considerable insight and judiciousness as a critic.

2. Throughout this study quotations from Hankin's dramas are taken from *The Plays of St. John Hankin*, ed. John Drinkwater, 2 vols. (London: Martin Secker, 1923).

3. Bernard Shaw, *The Man of Destiny*, in *Seven One-Act Plays*, (Baltimore: Penguin, 1958), pp. 47–48.

4. [A. B. Walkley], review of *The Two Mr. Wetherbys*, *Times Literary Supplement*, 20 March 1903, p. 90.

5. John Drew O'Neill, "The Comedy of St. John Hankin" (Ph.D. diss., University of Michigan, 1954), pp. 98–99.

6. Hankin, "A Note on Happy Endings," in *Dramatic Works*, 3: 126–27.

7. Oscar Wilde, *An Ideal Husband*, in *Oscar Wilde Plays*, (Harmondsworth, Middlesex, England: Penguin, 1970).

8. *The Serious Family*, adap. Morris Barnett (New York: Samuel French, n.d.).

3
"A Comedy for Fathers":
The Return of the Prodigal

When Hankin's second play[1] was staged in 1905, then revived in 1907, it faced a West-End rival in both title and subject, Hall Caine's *The Prodigal Son*. Caine's play was popular, both in its initial 1905 London run at the spacious Drury Lane—*the* theater for melodrama—and in its 1907 revival. *The Return of the Prodigal*, by way of contrast, was never a popular success, playing a modest number of performances in both 1905 and 1907 at the Court Theatre.

In *The Prodigal Son* Oscar returns home and wins the fiancée of his brother, Magnus. The second and third acts show Oscar busy prodigalizing: he becomes enamored of his sister-in-law, forges a bank note, is rejected by his father, and gets involved in a scheme to cheat an American senator of his winnings at a Riviera casino.

In the fourth and final act Oscar, who is unrecognized, returns to a farm where his mother, brother, and daughter, Elin, live. The next morning the farm is to be sold at auction since Magnus cannot pay his debts. Under the name of Christian Christiansson, Oscar has succeeded as a composer, lived in poverty and loneliness, and saved his earnings. At first he offers money if Elin is given to him for adoption. When Magnus and Elin refuse, Oscar leaves a pocketbook with Elin and asks that she give it to the sheriff. Later Elin produces the pocketbook, which is full of money, and all rejoice in the miracle.

In a brief postscript to the text, Caine wrote, "At the discretion of the Manager three further Tableaux may be added in the same Scene to typify the return and pardon of the prodigal."[2] The reviews of the original 1905 production suggest that such a happy ending was supplied.

By way of contrast, the plot of Hankin's *The Return of the Prodigal* has few complications and involves little action, most of that occurring in the last act. Set in the fictional town of Chedleigh, which "is famous for its cloth mills," the play centers on the Jackson and the Faringford families. The Jackson family—parvenus without rank—consists of Samuel Jackson, who owns a cloth mill and is standing for Parliament; Maria, his good-natured but fatuous wife; Violet, their dutiful, unmarried daughter; Henry, their industrious and successful son; and Eustace, the protagonist, a returned prodigal. The other family of the play, the Faringfords, who have rank and status but little money, consists of Sir John Faringford, Baronet, who is chairman of Mr. Jackson's election committee; Lady Faringford, his outspoken wife; and their docile daughter, Stella.

The exposition reveals that, after Eustace's numerous business failures, his father and his brother had shipped him off to Australia with 1,000 pounds. Five years later, at the time of the play begins, Eustace suddenly returns to his family's comfortable home, where he hopes to get a bed, food, and clothing. To gain a sympathetic admittance he shams illness. With the encouragement of Dr. Glaisher, whom Eustace easily fools, he ensconces himself in the Jackson home and, much to the irritation of Lady Faringford, flirts with her daughter, Stella, whom his brother Henry hopes to marry. After ten days of indolence and an admission from Eustace that he intends to do nothing, he is ordered from the house by Mr. Jackson. Eustace then blackmails Mr. Jackson and Henry by threatening to go to the local workhouse, thereby ruining both his father's chances for Parliament and his brother's chances for Stella. Three hours later Mr. Jackson and Henry offer Eustace another 1,000 pounds to return to Australia. Since Eustace considers the offer impractical—after all, he would only repeat his previous failures—he declines, then asks for a yearly allowance of 300 pounds. At first Mr. Jackson refuses then, after Henry points out that Eustace's plan is practical, agrees to an annual allowance of 250 pounds. Having successfully blackmailed his father and his brother, Eustace says that he gives up his claim to Stella and cheerfully leaves for London.

Caine's story is melodrama of the kind Hankin described in his earlier review of another Caine drama: plays that aim "to excite an emotion, not to imitate life. . . . Its characters are not human beings. . . . Unintelligible behavior is tolerated, even expected."[3] Thus, after Magnus overhears that his fiancée loves his prodigal brother, Oscar, and not himself,

> [MAGNUS *stops, his face changes, he reels and holds on to lintel with one hand and grips the dog by its collar with the other.* THORA *covers her face and sobs.* OSCAR *is carried away by her emotion. . . .* THORA *makes an inarticulate murmur, rises from her chair and turns away.* OSCAR *follows her, losing all control of himself.*]

The dialogue is only slightly more restrained than Caine's stage directions, and one can sense the aptness of Oscar Wilde's observation that Caine "wrote at the top of his voice."[4]

Although the two plays share the biblical story as background, the versions could scarcely be more different. Caine devotes much space to the prodigal's wanderings, whereas Hankin focuses on the events after the prodigal returns. Hankin's play is, in effect, a sequel to Caine's drama. A passage from *The Return of the Prodigal* at once suggests many differences between Caine and Hankin. In Hankin's version of clothing the returned prodigal, Mr. Jackson is stunned by a sizable bill from his tailor:

> EUSTACE [*whose energies are absorbed at the moment in blowing through cigarette-holder*]: They're mine, father.
> MR. JACKSON: What, sir!
> EUSTACE [*calmly*]: Some clothes I ordered. I told him to send the bill to you. That's all right, isn't it?

MR. JACKSON [*exploding*]: All right! Certainly not, sir. It's very far from right. It's a great liberty.

EUSTACE: My dear father, the bill must be sent in to somebody.

MR. JACKSON: And why not to you, pray?

EUSTACE: What would be the good of that, father. I've nothing to pay it with.

MR. JACKSON: Then you shouldn't have ordered the things.

EUSTACE: But I must wear something. I can't go on wearing Henry's things indefinitely. It's hard on *him*! [HENRY *snorts*.] My dear Henry!

Unlike Caine's drama and other conventional prodigal-son plays, Hankin's play depicts both the father and the elder son as self-centered, complacent, unforgiving, and unloving, while the younger, prodigal son remains unrepentant, lazy, and predatory; thus, the play lacks any happy ending reconciling prodigal and family. As in Shaw's *Arms and the Man* and *The Devil's Disciple* and many of Hankin's own earlier dramatic parodies, *The Return of the Prodigal* takes a potentially melodramatic situation and satirizes the conventional and comfortable. It has neither traditional morality nor theatrical sympathy.

Caine's play is reassuring and in general follows the biblical parable. Sin is punished and the prodigal comes home to do good deeds. Such events may take time, but God can work such miracles for the faithful if they follow the duty dictated by the older generation. Hankin's play is disturbing and repudiates the biblical parable, for it implies that life is vicious and competitive, with the wealthy and titled exploiting the weak, while Eustace in turn exploits the wealthy.

With *The Return of the Prodigal* Hankin began writing endings consistent with earlier characterizations and action. From this time on he rejected conventional "happy" endings, like those found in such late Victorian commercial plays as Henry Arthur Jones's *The Case of Rebellious Susan* (1894). Contrasting the endings of conventional plays with the conclusions of his own plays, Hankin in 1907 argued for lifelike endings:

I select an episode in the life of one of my characters or of
a group of characters, when something of importance to
their future has to be decided and I ring up my curtain. Having
shown how it was decided and why it was so decided, I ring
it down again. . . . It is the dramatist's business to represent
life, not to argue about it.

. . . The average conventional comedy . . . sends you out
of the theater with a tolerable certainty that half the marriages
which the author has so recklessly arranged during its progress
will turn out disastrous failures. My plays, on the contrary,
leave their characters at the fall of the curtain with a reasonable
prospect of happiness in the future. That is the most . . . that
can be asked of plays which represent life or try to do so.[5]

Unlike *The Two Mr. Wetherbys, The Return of the Prodigal* is true
to this credo; it ends neither with the engagement of Eustace
and Stella nor with an implausible reconciliation between Eustace
and his family. By so ending his play Hankin rejects—as he does
in his later plays—the Victorian notions of the ennobling power
of woman and marriage and the sanctity of the family.

Although the conclusion is a decided improvement over that
of Hankin's first play, the ending of *The Return of the Prodigal*
is marred. Late in the play Eustace "*very nearly losing his temper*"
says to his father, "Nobody *wants* to sponge on other people.
The idea's preposterous. We all *want* to be prosperous and highly
respected members of Society like you and Henry, with more
money than we know what to do with, with a seat in Parliament
and a wife out of the Baronetage. That's what we *want*. And
if we haven't the luck or the brains or the energy to get it, you
needn't call us names." Unlike many critics of the initial production who overgeneralized about the play's cynicism, Max Beerbohm
charged that Eustace is not tough-minded enough and that
the above speech is inconsistent with his character: "I have but
one fault to find. Eustace declares that of course he, like everyone
else, 'would *like* to be a highly respected, prosperous member
of the community.' I do not think that the true Eustace—the
widely typical Prodigal Son—would have felt that. He would

have had an innate aversion from respectability and prosperity. These things would have bored him, except perhaps for a while."[6] Eustace's speech *is* out of character. He would want to be a member of the wealthy middle class, not for the respectability, but for the pleasures and ease that life affords, as is implied by Eustace's speech to Henry, "Well, I think I'd change places with you. After all, you're pretty comfortable here. And you'll marry Stella, damn you!"

In *The Return of the Prodigal* Hankin satirizes the values of both parvenu manufacturers and impoverished aristocrats. The Jacksons exemplify the values of the Victorian commercial middle class, for whom "the struggle for money . . . was complemented, and to a considerable extent motivated, by the struggle for social advancement."[7] As Hankin's initial stage direction reveals, the Jacksons are parvenus with questionable taste and materialistic values: "*The* JACKSONS' *drawing-room, a handsome room suggesting opulence rather than taste. Not vulgar but not distinguished. Too full of furniture. . . . Too full of everything. . . . other inappropriate things.*" This wealth has been accumulated by mass production of an inferior product. As Mrs. Jackson tells Eustace, Henry has introduced planned obsolescence: "Henry said it was no use making cloth that would last a lifetime if people only wanted it to last twelve months. So he got over new machines—from America. And now they don't make any *good* cloth at all, and your father has trebled his income." Formerly, the Jacksons took pride in their craft and in the quality of their cloth. Now, their employees work overtime doing shoddy work.

With Lady Faringford, who is descended from Wilde's comic yet dominating and self-righteous ladies, Hankin criticizes aristocracy. In a set speech Lady Faringford emphasizes the survival of both the self-proclaimed elite and hierarchy:

> We were born into this world with what is called position. Owing to that position we are received everywhere, flattered, made much of. Though we are poor, rich people are eager to invite us to their houses and marry our daughters. So

much the better for us. But if we began telling people that position was all moonshine, family an antiquated superstition, and many duchesses far less like ladies than their maids, the world would ultimately discover that what we were saying was perfectly true. Whereupon we should lose the very comfortable niche in the social system which we at present enjoy, and—who knows?—might actually be reduced in the end to doing something useful for our living like other people. No, no, my dear, rank and birth and the peerage *may* be all nonsense, but it isn't *our* business to say so. Leave that to vulgar people who have something to gain by it. *Noblesse oblige!*

In this speech Hankin's voice breaks through—as it rarely does in his drama—to criticize those who get more out of life than they put into it. Elsewhere in the play Hankin also exposes Lady Faringford's indifference to suffering. Of her servants she casually volunteers, "Lamps are so troublesome. The servants are always setting themselves on fire with them." And of a Miss Higgs, a character mentioned in passing, Lady Faringford observes, "Fortunately, she was so affected by her loss [of her money] that she drowned herself in the canal at the bottom of her garden. Otherwise I'm afraid some sort of a subscription would have had to be got up for her." In a passage discussed below, Sir John Faringford is revealed as equally callous.

In common with many advanced Edwardian plays, *The Return of the Prodigal* criticizes unquestioning acceptance of rigid formulas for behavior, since they inhibit self-realization and pleasure.

Of the three Jackson children only Henry follows the family's codes. But Henry lacks vitality and humor; he lives by a rigid set of rules and values propriety and reputation more than feelings. Henry also seems to view Stella as a social advancement, not a person. Although not so intelligent as Eustace, Henry succeeds because he follows the Victorian virtues of duty and work—the latter word, as Walter E. Houghton pointed out, being "the most popular word in the Victorian vocabulary," with the exception of "God."[8] Unlike his brother, Eustace, the epitome

of non-Victorian values of idleness and levity, Henry is industrious
and somber. Furthermore, unlike Eustace, Henry holds a facile
view of growth and progress. Echoing his father's sense of duty
and doing his father's work, Henry is his father's son.

Sister Violet, by way of contrast, is aware of the futility and
injustice of her situation but is powerless to change it:

> I may sometimes get away for a few days, a week, perhaps,
> but very seldom. And as mother grows older I shall go less.
> Soon people will give up asking me when they find I always
> refuse. And so I shall be left here alone with no friends, no
> real companionship, merely one of the family obliged to
> know the people they know, visit the people they visit, not
> a grown woman with interests of her own and a life to order
> as she pleases. . . . What chance have I of marrying now?
> When we hadn't so much money, and Henry and father weren't
> so set on taking a position in the county, there was some
> chance for me. Now there is none. It's all very well for Henry.
> He is a partner in the firm. He will be a very rich man.
> He can marry Stella Faringford. Oh, we are to be great people!
> But you don't find Sir John Faringford's son proposing to
> *me*! No! He wants a girl of his own class or else an heiress,
> not a manufacturer's daughter with a few thousand pounds.
> So the great people won't marry me and I mustn't marry
> the little people. Father wouldn't like it. He hardly lets
> mother ask them to the house nowadays. And so the years go
> by and my youth with them, and I know it will be like this
> always, always.

Violet's plight, though, is not trumpeted. She is one of many
frustrated spinsters in Edwardian drama, but she is not depicted
in the usual way. Compared to the treatment of both the spinster
in *The Waters of Bitterness* (1903), who becomes so distraught
that she commits suicide, and the spinsters in *'Op o' Me Thumb*
(1904) and Joseph Conrad's *One Day More* (1905), who suffer
painful disillusionment, Hankin's depiction is restrained.
Violet neither commits suicide nor is disillusioned; she is neither

prominent in the play nor shown to suffer deeply. As elsewhere in his drama, here Hankin displays his distinctive, understated treatment of important subjects within the framework of comedy.

As a "cheery young man who does mean things with an air which defies and paralyses the moral judgment,"[9] Eustace belies his family's values of earnestness, work, and progress, as is seen in the mise-en-scène and stage business at the beginning of the third act. Here Eustace's nonchalance and independence contrast with Henry's gravity and industry:

> Ten days have passed since Act II. It is Saturday, and the time is after luncheon. . . . The lawn is bounded by a shrubbery, through which runs the path which HENRY had made three years previously to enable him to get to the mill quicker. When the curtain rises, EUSTACE is lying in a hammock, swinging lazily. He wears a new grey flannel suit, and looks exceedingly comfortable. Hard by, under a tree, are three or four wicker chairs, in one of which HENRY is sitting, reading the Market Report in "The Times." EUSTACE has a cup of coffee in his hand. HENRY has one on the table beside him. Presently EUSTACE drinks some, looking with indolent amusement at his brother absorbed in his newspaper.

Rejecting his family's inflexible codes of behavior, Eustace would rather drift, relax, enjoy, as Hankin advocated in his early essay "The True Sublime of Boating."

Eustace not only rejects traditional codes of behavior—as do other Hankin protagonists—he espouses the Darwinian view of natural selection, roughly the belief that nature allows only the best adjusted to survive. In the first decade of this century such an outlook was rare in English drama and unprecedented in a comedy:

> EUSTACE. . . . . There must be good cottages and bad cottages, in order that the strong may get the good cottages and the weak the bad.
> STELLA. You mean in order that the strong may have

the bad cottages and the weak the good. They need them more.

EUSTACE: That would be quite unscientific. No the strong must have the good cottages in order that they may grow stronger. And the weak must have the bad cottages in order that they may die off. Survival of the fittest, you know.

STELLA: How horrible!

EUSTACE: Yes, but how necessary!

In a world overpopulated by the likes of Mr. and Mrs. Simmonds (who do not appear on stage), predators and their victims struggle to survive. Eustace confides to Violet, "Henry and the governor [Mr. Jackson] I can stand up to. They're very much like me. We belong to the predatory type. Only they're more successful than I am. They live on their workpeople. I propose to live on them. We're birds of a feather." As Lady Faringford recounts it, Sir John Faringford has been a predator upon his tenants:

> One of his cottages . . . was let to young Barrett, quite a respectable, hard-working man—who afterwards died of pneumonia. Mr. Ling [who is running against Mr. Jackson for Parliament] declared the cottage was damp, and not fit for anyone to live in. . . . As if *all* cottages were not damp. The absurd part of it was that afterwards, when Mrs. Barrett was left a widow and Sir John gave her notice because she couldn't pay her rent, and he wanted to convert the cottage into pigsties, Mr. Ling was equally indignant, and seemed to think we ought to find Mrs. Barrett another house!

In the crowded and competitive world of *The Return of the Prodigal*, ill-adapted characters are inconsequential to those with wealth or status.

Elsewhere Eustace, sounding as if he has read Darwin *and* Zola, says that man lacks free will and that environment, chance, and heredity determine who survives:

> It's not what I do but what I am that is the difficulty. What does it matter what one *does*? It's done, and then

it's over and one can forget it. The real tragedy is what one
is. Because one can't escape from that. It's always there, the
bundle of passions, weakness, stupidities, that one calls character, waiting to trip one up. . . . Aren't we just the creatures
of our upbringing, of circumstance, of physical constitution?
We are launched on the stream at our birth. Some of us can
swim against the current. Those who can't it washes away.[10]

In another passage Eustace even goes so far as to say that man
should aid nature's course. With a bitter tone reminiscent of
Hankin's essay "The Criminal" (1893) and his short story "A
Man of Impulse" (1909), Eustace says to Mr. Jackson and Henry,

> We live in a humanitarian age. We coddle the sick and
> we keep alive the imbecile. We shall soon come to pensioning
> the idle and the dissolute. . . . England is covered with hospitals
> for the incurably diseased and asylums for the incurably
> mad. If a tenth of the money were spent on putting such
> people out of the world, and the rest were used in preventing
> the healthy people from falling sick, and the sane people
> from starving, we should be a wholesomer nation.

These lines also imply that only the fit should survive, but Eustace
in addition advocates that the English should intervene in
nature to insure that resources are not wasted in a futile attempt
to help the mentally and physically unfit. Instead, they should
be put "out of the world," so that resources could be used to
keep the survivors healthy.

As has been mentioned, like many Shavian plays, *The Return
of the Prodigal* inverts a potentially melodramatic situation
for satiric purposes. The play is also Shavian in its iconoclastic
hero. However, as Max Beerbohm pointed out, *The Return
of the Prodigal* is not the play Shaw would have written: "Mr.
Shaw, observing a prodigal son, would have knitted his brows,
outstretched his index finger, and harangued us to the effect
that the prodigal was perfectly right, as a citizen, in his refusal
to work under the present conditions of labo(u)r [*sic*], and

that these conditions are irrational, dangerous, and ought to be abolished. And this harangue would have been couched in the form of a delicious comedy."[11] In addition to being less didactic and reformist than Shaw, Hankin is also less affirmative. Unlike such Shavian plays as *Major Barbara*, also of 1905, *The Return of the Prodigal* stresses the force of heredity and environment and shows its protagonist's retreat from personal, social, and political problems.

In fact, Eustace's lack of achievements and plans has disquieted numerous critics. Perhaps Hankin gave Eustace neither will power nor progressive program because Hankin was plagued by loss of meaning and purpose, as is evident in his essays, and by his doubts about any "ism" improving man.[12] In his persuasive study of British ideas from 1880 to 1914, John A. Lester, Jr., observed, "By the late [nineteenth] century the web of circumstance had drawn in with finality. Man had been asked to sit down before the fact like a little child; he had for decades viewed with acquiescence and respect, and at times with exhilaration, the triumphs of science in the industrial age. Now the cosmology implicit in the new science began to assume coherence and came starkly into view. It revealed man helplessly enmeshed by inhuman and impersonal forces in a world he never made and could not control, caught up in a life of no purpose, neither human nor ethical nor divine."[13] Holding a comparable viewpoint, Hankin could offer fewer certainties than Shaw.

In spite of its subjects and themes, Hankin's play largely avoids the gloomy, earnest treatment of other serious plays of its time (such as Caine's rival drama), shuns close examination of specific social problems, and eschews the infectious, reformist zeal of Shaw. With *The Return of the Prodigal* Hankin found his distinctive voice: an amusing exposure of situations and characters by a rational yet pleasure-seeking protagonist, and a comic tone tinged with bitterness or melancholy. Hankin's second play is a curious hybrid of comedy of manners and Darwinian philosophy. It is marred by occasional lapses into embittered speechifying and by one of Eustace's passages that is out of character. The play has many admirable qualities, however. In *The Return of the Prodigal* Hankin gained in self-reliance: excluding Lady Faringford and Dr. Glaisher, the play's characters are more lifelike and less theatrical than the characters of *The Two Mr. Wetherbys*. In consistency and complexity of themes, the play shows an advancement over Hankin's first play as well. And in dealing with important subjects with insight and frequent humor, *The Return of the Prodigal* exhibits Hankin's approaching the maturity of his powers.

Notes

1. *The Return of the Prodigal* was first performed by the Court Theatre on 26 September 1905, and has been Hankin's most frequently revived play. Its most recent production was in London in 1973. (See Appendix C.)

2. Hall Caine, *The Prodigal Son* (London: [Ballantyne], 1905).

3. *Times* (London), 17 October 1899, p. 6.

4. A[lbert] E[dward] Wilson, *Edwardian Theatre* (London: Arthur Barker, 1951), p. 151.

5. St. John Hankin, "A Note on Happy Endings," in *The Dramatic Works of St. John Hankin,* ed. John Drinkwater (London: Martin Secker, 1912), 3: 120–21.

6. Max Beerbohm, "The Return of the Prodigal," *Saturday Review* 100 (7 October 1905): 464.

7. Walter E. Houghton, *The Victorian Frame of Mind* (New Haven: Yale University Press, 1957), p. 185.

8. Ibid., p. 242.

9. "The Stage from the Stalls," *Sketch* 51 (4 October 1905): 452.

10. This and many other references to drowning in Hankin's writings are interesting in light of his own suicide by drowning.

11. Beerbohm, p. 463.

12. Hankin to H. G. Wells, December 3 [1906], Rare Books Room, University of Illinois Library, Urbana.

13. John A. Lester, Jr., *Journey through Despair 1880–1914: Transformations in British Literary Culture* (Princeton: Princeton University Press, 1968), p. 24.

4
"A Comedy for Philanthropists":
The Charity that Began at Home

Hankin's third play was first performed by the Court Theatre in October of 1906 but has been out-of-print since 1914 and virtually unproduced since 1917. Such neglect is unfortunate. The play is amusing, genial, and effective satire.

Set in "Priors Ashton, Lady Denison's house in the country," where the titled and servants are prominent, the play takes place in a higher social class than that of *The Two Mr. Wetherbys* and *The Return of the Prodigal.* Act 1 introduces all of the characters and reveals that charitable activities consume the time of Lady Denison—who is fatuous, weak-willed, forgetful, but well-meaning—and Margery, her determined, idealistic daughter. Their mentor, Basil Hylton—the "Founder of the Church of Humanity"—is an overworked writer and preacher. His philosophy of giving people what they want, not what they deserve, is responsible for much of the play's action. Mrs. Eversleigh, Lady Denison's sister-in-law, is a selfish, candid, and opinionated commentator. Hugh Verreker, a guest at the Denisons', is the imperturbable, sensible, mildly hedonistic protagonist. Four other guests were invited because no one else will entertain them: Miss Triggs, a testy and brusque German governess; Firket, a salesman on commission, who leaves the Denisons during the one week interval between the first two acts; Mrs. Horrocks, a snobbish, quarrelsome lady, and General Bonsor, a retired Indian Army officer, who tells *"interminable stories."* Soon the footman tries to give notice because of the quarrelsome Soames, a butler with a record of thievery. Mrs. Eversleigh cannot fathom how anyone could turn a home "into a bear garden" out of altruism; so, she infers that Lady Denison is humoring the wealthy Hylton in order that he will marry Margery.

In the farcical second act complications multiply. Lady Denison who is burdened with trying to learn German to placate Miss Triggs, faces the following crises in rapid succession: General Bonsor and Mrs. Horrocks quarrel; the maid is found to be pregnant by Soames; he claims that he cannot marry her because he is already married; the General gets angry at Lady Denison; then Miss Triggs gets angry at her; and Margery announces her engagement to the impecunious Verreker—much to Lady Denison's and Mrs. Eversleigh's chagrin. Confused, Lady Denison rings to dismiss Soames.

In the next act, Lady Denison gets the unhappy news that the cook has given notice because of the scandal in the servants' quarters. Meanwhile, General Bonsor receives a letter revealing Verreker's shady past, and because Verreker has refused to humor the tiring General, he makes the contents of the letter known to Lady Denison. She and Mrs. Eversleigh confront Margery with the news about Verreker, but Margery reveals that he had disclosed his past to her before proposing and applying Hylton's philosophy argues that to keep Verreker from turning out badly she is determined to marry him. Then, without trying to excuse his action, Verreker recounts the questionable episode: to pay off gambling debts, he had taken from an army dining hall money that he could not repay before his commanding officer discovered it and demanded that Verreker resign his commission. Although Verreker says he will give up his claim to Margery if she wants him to, Margery insists that she will "stand by him." Shortly thereafter, Mrs. Eversleigh tells Verreker that the guests were invited because they were unworthy. To get even with the General for informing on him, Verreker tells the General that "Lady Denison selects her visitors on philanthropic grounds—because they're disagreeable or disreputable or merely boring." Mrs. Horrocks and Miss Triggs happen to overhear this disclosure, and, in spite of Lady Denison's flustered apologies, all three guests leave in a huff.

During the opening minutes of the final act the electric lights flash off and on, since Lady Denison has retained as manager of the dynamo an incompetent and intoxicated footman. For a week Verreker has tried to practice Margery's charity but now realizes that, although he and Margery are in love, they are mismatched and that Margery would be unhappy as Mrs. Verreker. Claiming to do the first nonselfish act of his life, he breaks off the engagement, tenderly kisses her goodbye, and suggests not unkindly that she marry Hylton, with whom she has much in common.

The Charity that Began at Home also touches upon the view of man as shaped largely by heredity and environment. Verreker argues briefly that personality traits are determined by the time of birth, and the guests reveal the shaping power of past experience and the difficulty of reforming behavior. Nonetheless, a comparison of *The Return of the Prodigal* and *The Charity That Began at Home* reveals that Darwinian survival of the fittest, an important theme in the former, is a muted theme in the latter. First, *The Charity that Began at Home* has no parasitic man acting in his own self-interest. Second, Verreker is no Darwinian spokesman. Finally, in contrast to *The Return of the Prodigal*—whose Miss Higgs and Mr. Barrett fall victim to the forces of nature—*The Charity that Began at Home* has no peripheral victims of environment. Instead, *The Charity that Began at Home* satirizes charitable and romantic idealism.

The Return of the Prodigal is Hankin's secular variation of the prodigal son motif; *The Charity that Began at Home* Hankin's variation of the Golden Rule.

MRS. EVERSLEIGH [*briskly*]: If people are disagreeable they don't deserve kindness.

HYLTON [*smiling*]: It's not what people *deserve* but what

they *want* that matters, don't you think? In fact, often the less people deserve the more we ought to help them. They need it more.

MRS. EVERSLEIGH: I'm afraid that's hardly a view you can expect me to take seriously, Mr. Hylton. It's very *modern* and original, but it's not *serious*.

HYLTON [*gently*]: I should hardly have called it *modern*. Usen't we to be taught that it was our duty to love our enemies?

MRS. EVERSLEIGH : Yes. But only on Sundays. And no one ever *dreamed* of doing it. So, of course, that didn't matter. You want Lady Denison to *do* it.

HYLTON [*more gravely*]: I certainly think the world would be a happier place and a better place if people helped each other because they needed help irrespective of whether they deserved it or not.

The first three acts are a *reductio ad absurdum* of Hylton's theories about charity. The consequences of applying his ideas are comic and clear: receivers of charity are an unreformable and ungrateful lot, whereas devoted practitioners of charity are idealists who discomfort both themselves and their recipients.

Ineffective charity was a frequent topic in such late Victorian and Edwardian plays as Pinero's *The Hobby-Horse* (1886), Jones's *The Crusaders* (1891), and Shaw's *Major Barbara* (1905). A comparison of *The Charity that Began at Home* with Jones's *The Crusaders* (1891) and Shaw's *Major Barbara* (1905) once again suggests Hankin's distinctive approach.

The Crusaders,[1] like Hankin's play, concerns both charity and romance. The action of this often amusing play shows the results of the London Reformation League to be "a revolution in South America, and two-pence on the income tax," as well as blighted roses and scandal at the league's Wimbledon rose farm. The love triangle of Cynthia Greenslade, a widow whose doddering husband left his wealth to Philos Ingarfield's reformation efforts; Ingarfield, "Something between an angel, a fool, and a poet, And atrociously in earnest! A sort of Shelley from

Peckham Rye"; and Dick Rusper, a nonreformer devoted to Cynthia, is finally and abruptly resolved with a Cynthia-Philos match.

Charitable reformers are treated much as they are in Hankin's plays: as naive and ineffectual or unwittingly destructive. "The comedy does preserve, exaggerated to be sure as in caricature, a picture of the large leisured class enriched by industry or rents who succumbed to the fashion of playing at charity, but who had no scientific knowledge of social questions, their ignorance usually leading to ultimate aggravation of conditions as in *The Crusaders*."[2] In the last moments of the play, however, the audience/reader witnesses the match of Philos, who has been shown as foolish and inept, and Cynthia, a thinly drawn, implausible character. It's a wonder Hankin never wrote a dramatic sequel to the play. Hankin's characterizations of Hylton, Margery, and Verreker are more convincing than Jones's and their actions consistent with their characterizations, thus the Verreker-Margery disengagement and Hankin's "happy ending."

Both *Major Barbara* and *The Charity that Began at Home* expose the impracticality of certain kinds of charity, but Hankin's play lacks Shaw's suggestions about economic causes and cures. *Major Barbara* ends with the education (and engagement) of Barbara and Cusins and with the prospect of personal and economic growth; *The Charity that Began at Home* ends with the characters unchanged and its protagonist disengaged. Hankin's play has neither the implausible romantic conclusion of Jones's play, nor the reformist zeal of Shaw's; rather, it reveals again Hankin's distinctive amused and commonsensical presentation of unreformable folly.

The last act of *The Charity that Began at Home* shows the strains on a mismatched couple and concludes on a note of civility, reason, and disengagement. In contrast to a long tradition in comedy, at least as old as Aristophanes, Hankin always refused to end his comedies with marriages. *The Charity that Began at Home*, developing a theme of *The Two Mr. Wetherbys*, argues that reason should control passion. Verreker, for example, confides to Margery, "Let's face facts, and not shirk them as every one else seems to do. Marriage isn't a thing to be romantic about. It *lasts* too long. . . . As one marries for a long time one should choose carefully, reasonably. One mustn't be carried away by passion. Passion's a great thing in marriage, but common sense is a greater." Verreker attempts to subordinate common sense to passion: for a week he practices Margery's charity. But he passes the ultimate test of reason by seeing that he must be true to himself and not make unhappy the woman he loves. In championing reason over sentiment, Verreker reacts to the Victorian notion that love and marriage reform man. Verreker does not think that man can change, and he could not agree with Hylton that "there's nothing the love of a really good woman can't do for a man. It brings out all that is fine in his nature, and drives out all that is base. That is what your marriage will do for you."

The Two Mr. Wetherbys shows the difference between Robert Carne's life of duty and Richard Wetherby's enjoyable, carefree ways. In *The Return of the Prodigal* Henry and Eustace are similarly contrasted. *The Charity that Began at Home* also plays a variation on this theme; says Verreker to Margery, "You look on life as a moral discipline. I look on it as a means to enjoyment. You think only of doing what you imagine to be right. I think only of getting what I know to be pleasant." Like Richard Wetherby and Eustace, the easygoing and healthy Verreker seeks pleasure, not sacrifice: "They say some forms of suffering ennoble people, and putting up with what one doesn't like is supposed to be good for the character–though I'm sure I don't know why." In contrast to Lady Denison, Margery, and Hylton–who are all usually too diligent to relax–Verreker can reject the Victorian ideals of earnestness and duty and can enjoy himself; indeed, he sees little reason to do anything else. Furthermore, unlike all the other characters in *The Charity that Began at Home*, Verreker can laugh at himself. After Mrs. Eversleigh informs Verreker why he was invited, he "*bursts into a shout of delighted laughter. . . . [laughs again.]* How delicious! So *that's* why I was invited! Because

I was down on my luck and wasn't asked to many houses! And I thought it was because of my delightful society."

In the Shavian manner, *The Charity that Began at Home* undercuts earnest idealists, dreamers or theorizers, and approves of insouciant realists, those who learn from experience and act upon that understanding. Similar to such Shavian idealists as Barbara and the Reverend Morell, Hylton has too great faith in the power of words. He overestimates the effects of his preaching and writing, and he hypothesizes, "It's wonderful how a little kindness and goodwill soften people"; yet the consequences of his kindness and goodwill, such as the maid's pregnancy, reduce him to ineffectuality: "As things stand, I'm afraid there's nothing to suggest. We must do our best for this poor girl, of course, [*more sternly*] and Soames must help us in any way he can. That's all I can think of." Margery is naive too. Early in the play she tells the footman, "Things always go better if only one tries to *help* people, don't they?" yet after numerous tribulations, at the end of act 3 occurs an exodus of "helped" guests. The play demonstrates that the preaching, writing, kindness, and goodwill of idealists cannot help selfish and unchangeable people. The realist Verreker admits that he is "selfish and isn't at all ashamed of it. . . . [and that] ideals do more harm than good," and finally washes his hands of the likeable but misguided idealists.

Unlike the plays of Shaw and Barker (*The Voysey Inheritance*, for example), Hankin's plays show neither education nor reformation of idealists. Growth and rewards are foreign to Hankin's plays because he did not share Shaw's and Barker's optimism that people can change. Also Hankin does not argue for improving the world. In fact, usually the pre–World War I domain of Hankin's plays is not all that unpleasant unless, like Margery, one *feels* too much:

MARGERY [*horrified*]: Mr. Verreker, you *can't mean* that! You must feel sometimes how splendid it would be to do something heroic, to lay down your life for a great cause, to make the world better.

VERREKER [*laughing*]: I don't want to make the world better. I think the world's all right as it is.

MARGERY [*astonished*]: But you can't *always* feel like that? There must be times when you feel that the world is full of suffering and injustice. That it's not all right, but all wrong.

VERREKER [*refusing to be impressed*]: Oh yes. When I'm not well, you mean?

MARGERY [*hurt*]: No, I don't. Seriously.

VERREKER [*thinks for a moment*]: Well, sometimes, perhaps—when I'm with *you*, for instance—I have a dim feeling that if we all put our backs into it we might improve things. But I struggle against it.

MARGERY [*wondering*]: Why struggle against it—if you think it would make things better?

VERREKER: Because people who try to improve the world have rather an uncomfortable time, Miss Denison. And I've a great dislike of being uncomfortable.

Verreker and Margery illustrate again the Walpole epigraph Hankin quoted on the title page of his first play, "*Life is a comedy to those who think, a tragedy to those who feel.*" In contrast to such Shavian heroes as Andrew Undershaft and such Jones reformers as Philos Ingarfield and Cynthia Greenslade, Hugh Verreker is blithely satisfied with the world. More so than *The Return of the Prodigal, The Charity that Began at Home* fits Hankin's claim to cool observation of life and follows Hankin's own dictum that "it is the dramatist's business to represent life, not to argue about it."[3] Thus, Verreker is a less philosophical and less angry protagonist than Eustace; the tone of *The Charity that Began at Home* is less bitter than that of *The Return of the Prodigal*; and *The Charity that Began at Home* is less didactic as well.

The central conflicts of Hankin's first two plays tend to be one-sided, with little substance given to the opponents of Hankin's heroes. However, *The Charity that Began at Home* balances the central conflict of idealists and realists more evenly. In contrast to Hankin's targets of satire in earlier plays, Hylton is portrayed in a mellow light. He is sympathetic, even compassionate to Verreker, and the latter cannot dismiss Hylton as a mere fool:

> HYLTON: The age of miracles will never pass while there are men and women like Miss Denison in the world!
> [*The utter sincerity with which* HYLTON *says this makes it impossible to laugh at him, even good-naturedly, as* VERREKER *would like to do.* HYLTON, *with the glow in his face and the look of the mystic in his eyes, is not a man one can laugh at, while his absolute unconsciousness, his total lack of anything like pose or insincerity, makes* VERREKER *feel that he has never liked him or admired him so much before. It may be madness, but it is a divine madness. There is silence between them for a moment while* VERREKER *looks at his companion curiously. Then a slow smile comes into his face, and he speaks quietly.*]
> VERREKER: You're a queer chap, Hylton.
> HYLTON [*returning to ordinary life with a start*]: Why?
> VERREKER [*thinking better of it*]: Nothing.

In this scene Hankin displayed a subtlety and resonance of characterization found only in *The Constant Lover*. Probably Verreker speaks for Hankin when he says Hylton is "an excellent chap but quite mad," and the epigraph to the play, *"The souls of the just are in the hands of God,"* is not entirely ironic. As Hankin elsewhere wrote of Hylton, "There is a providence which watches over good people and fools, and they never come up to really serious grief."[4]

Mrs. Eversleigh is complex too: she is both an object of satire, insofar as she is snobbish and stern, and an astute commentator on the foolishness of others. Although the minor characters— Firket, Mrs. Horrocks, and General Bonsor—are stock types, *The Charity that Began at Home* displays greater subtlety in characterization and conflict than Hankin's earlier plays. Mrs. Eversleigh and Hylton are rendered more deftly and more sympathetically than their earlier counterparts: Clara and Robert

Carne in *The Two Mr. Wetherbys* and Lady Faringford, Mr. Jackson, and Henry in *The Return of the Prodigal.*

The Charity that Began at Home is Hankin's first play with a completely uncompromising ending and a protagonist who always speaks in character. Thus *The Charity that Began at Home* does not undermine its hero's ideas, his preference for common sense over romanticism; realism over idealism; genteel hedonism over moral discipline; and selfishness over charity. In other words, *The Charity that Began at Home* has greater consistency of character and greater thematic unity than either of Hankin's first two plays. Hankin's third play also has complex portraits of its antagonists, more balanced conflict, and virtually no didacticism. It is also quite amusing. Granville Barker and Hankin himself rated *The Charity that Began at Home* as Hankin's best play.[5] Only *The Constant Lover* rivals it for that honor.

Notes

1. Henry A. Jones, *The Crusaders,* in *Representative Plays,* ed. Clayton Hamilton, vol. 2 (Boston: Little, Brown, 1925). The play was first printed in 1892.

2. Richard A. Cordell, *Henry Arthur Jones and the Modern Drama* (New York: Ray Long & Richard R. Smith, 1932), p. 100.

3. St. John Hankin, "A Note on Happy Endings," in *The Dramatic Works of St. John Hankin,* ed. John Drinkwater (London: Martin Secker, 1912), 3: 121.

4. Ibid., p. 128.

5. "In the Days of my Youth," *M.A.P.* 22 (10 April 1909): 349. This interview is reprinted in Appendix B.

St. John Hankin in 1907, at age thirty-seven

5

"A Comedy for Mothers":
The Cassilis Engagement

During its initial February 1907 production by the Stage Society, Hankin's penultimate full-length comedy received tepid reviews and had a short run. After his death, *The Cassilis Engagement* was popular with repertory theaters in the provinces (see Appendix C). In 1917 one reviewer wrote that with Birmingham Repertory Theatre audiences "its only rival in familiarity and favour is 'The Importance of Being Earnest.' "[1] By 1923 it was the most often-performed play in Birmingham Repertory Theatre history. Between 1913 and 1926, that group produced the play at least ten different times, and it inevitably received rave reviews. Since 1926, however, the play has been only rarely revived.

The story is set in a higher social level than is *The Return of the Prodigal* and *The Charity that Began at Home*:

> The Jacksons . . . knew and consorted with the neighboring gentry; but the Denisons are gentry itself. . . . In Mrs. Cassilis' Deynham Abbey the social tone is even richer and more high-bred than that of Priors Ashton [of *The Charity that Began at Home*]. Her sister is Lady Marchmont; their neighbors and friends are the Countess of Remenham and her daughter, the Lady Mabel. *Her* drawing-room is "very handsome" and done in Louis Seize. She has twelve thousand pounds a year and is dressed (exquisitely) by Clarice. Terraces, strawberry-

beds, greenhouses, billiard rooms, smoking rooms, and morning rooms exist in apparent profusion. (Bedrooms do not
figure in Hankin's kind of comedy.) All this, of course, complete with the necessary staff. The Cassilises are indubitable
quality and have been so for a long time.[2]

To protect this aristocratic terrain from a young Cockney woman
engaged to her naive son, Mrs. Cassilis uses her acumen and
self-control.

The action of the play is so simple that an act by act plot
summary is unnecessary. Geoffrey Cassilis, the only and spoiled
child of his devoted mother, has become engaged to the attractive Ethel Borridge, much to the delight of her opportunistic
mother. (In the course of the play we learn that Mrs. Borridge
had lived with Mr. Borridge before they were married; Mr.
Borridge had drunk himself into his grave; Mrs. Borridge had
failed to get her daughter married to the rich, old, already-married
Lord Buckfastleigh; and the other Borridge daughter had become
a prostitute.) Both Lady Marchmont, who is Mrs. Cassilis'
sister, and the Cassilis' neighbors—the Reverend and Mrs. Herries
and the outspoken Countess of Remenham—are shocked by
Geoffrey's engagement and think Mrs. Cassilis has lost her
senses because she does not forbid it. Although Mrs. Cassilis
vehemently opposes the engagement, she hides her feelings
from all but Lady Marchmont and encourages a prolonged
visit of the Borridges. Mrs. Cassilis also invites both the Countess
of Remenham's disreputable brother, Major Warrington, who
she thinks might win Ethel from Geoffrey, and Lady Mabel
Venning, the Countess of Remenham's daughter and Geoffrey's
friend since childhood. Mrs. Cassilis hopes that, if she does
not openly oppose her son's will and if she encourages him
to visit with both Mabel and Ethel and her vulgar mother,
then Geoffrey will eventually realize his error and break off
the engagement. After the Borridges visit with the Cassilises
and their friends and relatives for a week, Ethel is so bored and
irritated that she first proposes a trip to Paris with Major Warring-

ton, then breaks off the engagement with Geoffrey, and, in spite of her mother's outburst, departs for London.

Like its two predecessors in *Three Plays with Happy Endings, The Cassilis Engagement* has an ending consistent with its premises, but "unhappy" by traditional dramatic standards. This "Comedy for Mothers" ends not with engagements, marriages, and celebrations but with the disengagement of Ethel and Geoffrey and the triumph of the gloating, snobbish Countess of Remenham. The play shows the events leading to a disengagement rather than the consequences or reactions to it; Hankin refuses to hint at either what happens next or what the characters *think* about the outcome of the events. Ethel leaves, and in the background Geoffrey scowls and says nothing: he *"is too depressed to notice anything."*

Whereas Hankin's heroes had been charming and outspoken, his first heroine is charming and devious. Mrs. Cassilis confides to Lady Marchmont: "I do it because I must, because it's the only way to save Geoffrey. If Geoffrey married her he'd be miserable, and I won't have that. Of course it would be *pleasanter* to be perfectly straightforward, and tell the girl I detest her. But if I did she'd marry Geoff if only to spite me. So I must trap her as she has trapped him. It's not a *nice* game, but it's the only possible one." Mrs. Cassilis is poised, intelligent, and selfish, and her action is guided by common sense, not feelings. However, unlike previous Hankin protagonists, because of her situation she is frank only with her confidante, Lady Marchmont, and she's neither hedonistic nor insouciant.

These qualities are embodied in Major Algernon Warrington—although his reputation exceeds his deeds. When propositioned by Ethel, Major Warrington beats a hasty retreat: "[*shaking himself free, desperately*]. My dear young lady, haven't I just told you that I'm not that sort at all? I'm a perfectly respectable person, of rather austere morality than otherwise." Here, as in many Shavian and earlier plays, woman is the pursuer, man the pursued. Warrington's conflict with his sister, the blue-blooded Countess of Remenham, is once again that of undutiful, insouciant, and mildly hedonistic man with conventional and authoritative woman. But this opposition is of only minor importance, since Warrington appears in just one act.

Nor is Mrs. Cassilis a commentator. Instead, she is a mother dedicated to disengaging her foolish son. What Barbara Bellow Watson said of Candida, "Here is the motherly woman again, placing that role above passion, romance and even independence,"[3] is often exemplified in Victorian and Edwardian drama. Such Edwardian plays as S. M. Fox's *The Waters of Bitterness* (1903), Hope Merrick's *Jimmy's Mother* (1905), Hankin's own *The Return of the Prodigal* (1905), Shaw's *Man and Superman* (1905) and Frederick Fenn's *The Convict on the Hearth* (1906) all attest to the Edwardian preoccupation with motherhood. *The Cassilis Engagement*, which is subtitled "A Comedy for Mothers," has three devoted mothers: the Countess of Remenham, Mrs. Borridge, and Mrs. Cassilis. Mrs. Borridge seems to live only for the welfare of her daughter, Ethel. And with Mrs. Cassilis and Geoffrey, Hankin depicts a passion that he never shows between lovers:

> MRS. CASSILIS: Looks mean so much to a man, don't they? And he [Geoffrey] has always admired me. Now I shall want him to admire me more than ever.
> LADY MARCHMONT: Why, dear?
> MRS. CASSILIS [*with cold intensity*]: Because I have a rival.

Mrs. Cassilis then explains how she will encourage the death of Geoffrey's and Ethel's infatuation:

> So it dies. [*With a bitter smile*]. *My* place is by its deathbed.
> LADY MARCHMONT [*with a slight shudder*]: That sounds rather ghoulish.
> MRS. CASSILIS: It *is*.

In this passage and in passages lighter in tone Hankin displays a deft rendition of mother Cassilis.

Once again Hankin is no reformer. *The Cassilis Engagement* touches upon the Borridges' economic difficulties, but the play does not *show* the exploitation of the lower class. Instead, it reveals in what ways the lower class is incompatible with the aristocracy: the Borridges and Cassilises differ most in language, social conduct, and pastimes. These differences are most evident during an evening gathering. After Mabel sings two verses of a Schubert lied to the assembled guests, Ethel is persuaded to sing, and she breaks into a lusty rendition of an off-color, music-hall ditty: "Stop that, Joey! Stow it, Joe!/Stop that ticklin' when I tell yer toe./You're too free to suit a girl like me,/Just you stop that ticklin' or I'll slap yer! . . ." Near the end of her song, she

[*Sings chorus fortissimo, joined by her delighted mother and by* WARRINGTON, *who beats time sonorously on the top of the piano. For this attention she slaps him cordially on the cheek at the last line, by way of giving an artistic finish to the situation, and then rises, flushed and excited, and stands by the piano, looking defiantly at her horrified audience.*]

WARRINGTON: Splendid, by Jove! Capital!

[*That, however, is clearly not the opinion of the rest of the listeners, for the song has what is called a "mixed" reception. The ladies, for the most part, had originally settled themselves into their places prepared to listen to anything which was set before them with polite indifference. A few bars, however, suffice to convince them of the impossibility of that attitude.* LADY REMENHAM, *who is sitting on the sofa by* LADY MARCHMONT, *exchanges a horrified glance with that lady, and with* MRS. HERRIES *on the other side of the room.* MABEL *looks uncomfortable. The* RECTOR *feigns abstraction.* MRS. CASSILIS *remains calm and sweet, but avoids every one's eye, and more particularly* GEOFFREY'S *who looks intensely miserable. But* WARRINGTON *enjoys himself thoroughly, even down to the final slap, and as for* MRS. BORRIDGE, *her satisfaction is unmeasured. She beats time to the final chorus, wagging her old head and joining in in stentorian accents, finally jumping up from her chair, clapping her hands, and crying, "That's right, Eth. Give 'em another." . . . Suddenly, however, she becomes conscious of the horrified silence which surrounds her. The cheers die away on her lips. She looks round the room, dazed and almost frightened, then hurriedly reseats herself in her chair, from which she has risen in her excitement, straightens her wig, and—there is an awful pause.*]

While revealing again his awareness of the visual expressiveness of drama, Hankin amusingly shows the incompatibility of two classes.

Thus, the play affirms motherhood, the caste system, and marriages within the same class. The drama also suggests that life-style is an expression of class rather than individual temperament and that life-style is unalterable. Differences between a proletarian and an aristocrat are simply not obliterated by marriage.

By way of contrast, T. W. Robertson's *Caste* (1867)[4]—still well known in London by the time of *The Cassilis Engagement*[5]—suggests that successful marriages between members of different classes may occur. Both *Caste* and *The Cassilis Engagement* show a rich man misallied with a penniless woman whose disreputable parent is a glaring reminder of the couple's difference in background, interests, and rank. However, by suggesting that Esther, the lower-class heroine, is untouched by the restrictions of caste, Robertson leaves unexplored the more frequent problem of the *un*exceptional lower-class character.

At least as early as 1899 Hankin had criticized *Caste*, in an unsigned review of a revival of that play.[6] Two years later, in a brief preface to his sequel to *Caste*,[7] Hankin commented, "If the perusal of the following scene prevents any young subaltern from emulating *D'Alroy* and marrying a ballet-dancer with a drunken father, it will not have been written in vain." Like Hankin's sequel to Lytton's *The Lady of Lyons*, his sequel to *Caste* shows in-law (and other) problems: D'Alroy's mother, the Marchioness, continues to think Mr. Eccles and the Gerridges (Esther's sister and brother-in-law) undesirable company and is unreconciled to Esther's marriage to her son. D'Alroy has

been asked to resign his commission in the army because his
father-in-law frequently showed up drunk at the mess-room;
Eccles "made his hundred and fifty-sixth appearance in the
police court last week. The fact was made the subject of jocular
comment in the cheaper evening papers," and since he has
taken lodging nearby, he is a frequent intoxicated visitor to the
D'Alroys. Visiting with the Gerridges narrows the D'Alroys'
circle of acquaintances, and little George D'Alroy by playing
with the Gerridge children is acquiring a Cockney accent.

Both in his sequel to *Caste* and in *The Cassilis Engagement*
Hankin dwells upon those aspects which Robertson's play
slights, particularly the considerations of the relatives and friends
of one partner of the couple getting along with the relatives
and friends of the other. In his sequel to *Caste* Hankin amusingly
displays the incessant quarreling caused by a misalliance. In
The Cassilis Engagement some of the potential problems of a
misalliance are depicted. The emotional scene of D'Alroy's
reunion with his wife, the concluding noble speeches, and
the tableau of two beaming families is replaced by the scene
of Ethel breaking off her engagement, then leaving Geoffrey
to his aristocratic life.

Hankin's treatment of caste is much closer to that of one
of Somerset Maugham's earliest plays, *Loaves and Fishes*,[8] which
was written in 1902 but was unstaged until 1911. It is impossible
to say if Hankin had seen Maugham's play in manuscript, yet
the parallels between Maugham's and Hankin's plays are striking.

Loaves and Fishes contains two plot lines. In one, Canon
Spratte proposes to a rich widow, but she outfoxes him by telling
him that her income ceases when she remarries, so he proposes
to the young, rich girl friend of his own son and is accepted
by her. In the other segment of the plot, Canon Spratte manip-
ulates his daughter, Winnie, out of an engagement to Christian-
Socialist Railing and into an engagement with a man of her
own class, Lord Wroxham. The Canon achieves his goal by
seeming to approve of the match of Winnie and Railing and
by encouraging visits by both Railing's vulgar mother and

Railing's sister, Louise, a hostile, defensive, outspoken suffragist and radical. Winnie then sees her error, breaks off the match, and accepts Lord Wroxham.

Like Mrs. Cassilis, Canon Spratte feigns acceptance of a proposed alliance of a naive upper-class child with a lower-class partner, then encourages visiting with the lower-class family of the fiancé(e) in order to break off the engagement. Both plays advocate alliances within one's own class. Nonetheless, Hankin is more sympathetic to the lower classes than Maugham. In Hankin's play, Ethel breaks off the match and does so with firmness and kindness. By way of contrast, Maugham gives no saving grace to Mrs. Railing and Louise, and Winnie, not Railing, does the rejecting. While advocating marriages within one's class, Hankin, compared to Maugham, gives a more equitable, less snobbish, and more amusing presentation of class differences.

In Hankin's play the country aristocrats fare little better than the city proletarians. The Countess of Remenham is nosey, opinionated, and intimidating; Geoffrey is insipid; Mrs. Cassilis is admirable—but not flawless. Such stage directions indicating that Mrs. Borridge is *"a beaming, good-natured harridan for all that. As a landlady you would rather like her"* suggest that Hankin attempted to be fair in depicting her, but with her Hankin is most open to the charge of snobbishness. Mrs. Cassilis and Lady Marchmont so often and so easily fool Mrs. Borridge and make fun of her, and the disreputable Borridge background is exaggerated. Ethel, however, is quite appealing. She shows pluck and insight, and she is independent and assertive, refusing to be "dutiful" to her opportunistic mother; furthermore, like Verreker of *The Charity that Began at Home*, she is firm yet kind in ending an intolerable engagement. Although she has a disreputable past and lacks the shrewdness and self-control of Mrs. Cassilis, Ethel is more sympathetic than the other characters of her age, Geoffrey and Mabel, and on balance is highly admirable.

To its favor, the themes of *The Cassilis Engagement* are consistently, persuasively, and for the most part entertainingly presented, and Ethel and Mrs. Cassilis, two members of different classes, are deftly characterized. To the play's discredit, Mrs. Cassilis sometimes explains to her confidante material that an alert viewer/reader should discover, and although the play's premise is imaginative, Ethel's growing boredom sometimes becomes tedious to witness. In addition several characters are incompletely realized. Geoffrey's role, as virtually all reviewers have noted, is thinly written: he is stupid, vain, and insensitive. And as one critic of the original production concluded,

Although produced under the auspices of a society which claims to represent advanced thought and real observation of life, so many of the characters do and say things obviously for effect, and not as the outcome of their temperaments. For instance, the parson is a conventional stage parson, the old aunt is a conventional society aunt, and, above all, the part of Mrs. Borridge is so heavily over-coloured, that one cannot believe the author to have studied from the life. Mr. Hankin has done better work than this, and he should beware lest the desire for popular success lead him into paths where such wit and power of characterisation as are his will be wasted.[9]

Unfortunately, since 1926 producers have justifiably neglected *The Cassilis Engagement.*

Notes

1. "The Repertory Theatre," *Birmingham Post*, 17 September 1917, p. 2, col. 7.

2. John Drew O'Neill, "The Comedy of St. John Hankin" (Ph.D. diss., University of Michigan 1954), pp. 125–26.

3. Barbara Bellow Watson, *A Shavian Guide to the Intelligent Woman* (London: Chatto & Windus, 1964), p. 123.

4. T. W. Robertson, *Caste*, in *Nineteenth-Century Plays*, ed. George Rowell (London: Oxford University Press, 1965), p. 405.

5. Reviews of *The Cassilis Engagement* in *Times Literary Supplement*, 15 February 1907,

p. 54; *Athenaeum*, no. 4138 (16 February 1907), p. 207; and *Saturday Review* 103 (16 February 1907): 199–200 all refer to *Caste*.

6. *Times* (London), 20 March 1899, p. 3.

7. St. John Hankin, "The Vengeance of Caste," *Punch* 120 (27 February 1901): 162, 164; reprint ed. in *Mr. Punch's Dramatic Sequels* (London: Bradbury, Agnew, [1901]) and in *Dramatic Sequels* (London: Martin Secker, 1925 or 1926; New York: Minton, Balch, 1926).

8. W. Somerset Maugham, *Loaves and Fishes*, in *Edwardian Plays*, ed. Gerald Weales (New York: Hill & Wang, 1962).

9. "Theatres," *Truth* 61 (20 February 1907): 451.

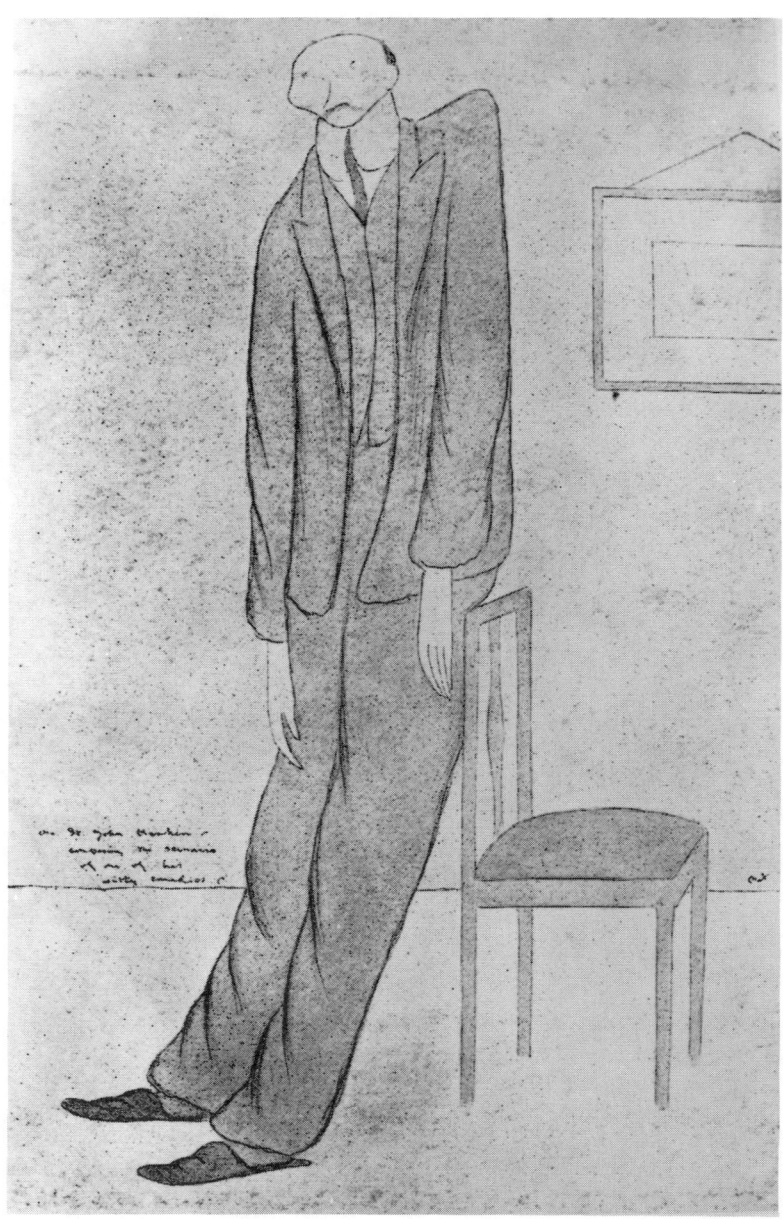

A Max Beerbohm Caricature, "Mr. St. John Hankin Composing the Scenario of One of his Witty Comedies."

6
"A Play without a Preface":
The Last of the De Mullins

In the 3rd Act Lillah [McCarthy, the lead actress in the original Stage Society production] appealed with extraordinary gusto to every unmarried woman of twenty-eight in the house to go straight out and procure a baby at once without the slightest regard to law or convention. As Lillah regards this a most obvious and reasonable doctrine, she had no idea of the effect she was producing in the audience. At the end of the Act the majority were simply afraid to applaud: the thing had gone quite beyond mere play-acting for them, and although they were interested, they felt–quite rightly–that to clap such sentiments would be to vote for them. Consequently, though there were curtain calls, they were forced by a partly friendly, partly assenting minority. Anything like a hit in the ordinary uproarious way was quite out of the question. The play will have to fight its way like A Doll's House.[1]

So wrote Bernard Shaw to Granville Barker shortly after the first performance of Hankin's last full-length play in December of 1908. Indeed, *The Last of the De Mullins* has had to fight its way with the critics as with its first audience. Although some commentators see it as Hankin's best play–in which "cynicism" is replaced by a ringing philosophy and an aloof protagonist is replaced by a rousing one–numerous critics have charged Hankin with unwise subordination of characterization to thesis, with the creation of a protagonist who is merely the author's shrill *raison-neuse,* and finally with a kind of drama alien to Hankin's bent.

Like *The Cassilis Engagement, The Last of the De Mullins* takes place among country gentry. The initial stage direction of the play—always significant in Hankin's dramas for establishing the social world—reveals a family comfortably steeped in tradition and position:

> SCENE.—*The Inner Hall at the Manor House in Brendon-Under-wood village. An old-fashioned, white-panelled room. At the back is a big stone-mullioned Tudor window looking out on to the garden. . . . The furniture is oak, mostly Jacobean or older. The righthand wall of the room is mainly occupied by a great Tudor fire-place, over which the De Mullin coat-of-arms is carved in stone. . . . The walls are hung with a long succession of family portraits of all periods and in all stages of dinginess as to both canvas and frame.*

The De Mullins are proud that their ancestors have lived in this house in Brendon, Dorset, for 400 years.

During the action of the play, which covers ten days, a young, unmarried woman returns home with her illegitimate son, quarrels with her aristocratic family, then leaves to return to her trade in London. Over eight years before the play's opening, Janet De Mullin had gotten pregnant and had gone to London. There, under the guise of widowhood and a new name, she had used an aunt's legacy to go into partnership in a hat shop. At the play's opening, the attractive thirty-six-year-old Janet has been summoned home by her mother, fearful that Mr. De Mullin was near death. After Janet returns with her eight-year-old-son, Johnny, she is accepted back by her family, consisting of her father, Hugo De Mullin, who *"looks weak and pale and altogether extremely sorry for himself, obviously a nervous and a very tiresome patient"*; her mother, Mrs. De Mullin, *"a crushed, timid creature of fifty-eight or so, entirely dominated by the* DE MULLIN *fetish and quite unable to hold her own against either her husband or her sister-in-law. . . . For the rest, a gentle, kindly lady, rather charming in her extreme helplessness"*; her younger sister, Hester, *"a lean, angular girl of twenty-eight, very plainly and unattractively dressed in sombre tight-fitting clothes"*; and her opinionated aunt, Mrs. Clouston, *"a hard-mouthed, resolute woman of sixty."*

In the second act Monty Bulstead discovers that he had fathered Janet's child and says that, had he known, he would have offered to marry Janet. She, however, says she would have rejected a proposal made out of "duty." Later Janet tells her mother that she would not spend the rest of her life with such an uninteresting man and that she is unlikely to marry at all.

In the third and final act, Mr. De Mullin and his sister, Mrs. Clouston, express disapproval of Janet's independence, of her running a shop, and of Johnny's growing up without esteem for the De Mullin ancestry. To prevent the family name from dying out, Mr. De Mullin volunteers to adopt Johnny. When Mr. De Mullin asks, then demands, that Janet and Johnny return home and live with the De Mullins, Janet, who has been irritated and bored with her family's life-style, refuses her father's demand, denounces the sterility of her family's way of life, and proclaims the value of her work. Mr. Brown, the curate whom Hester had hoped to marry, has proposed to Monty Bulstead's sister because Janet's return spoiled Hester's chances, but Janet urges her sister to live fully and to make the best of her youth by marrying the next curate and by having children. After a passionate speech on the joys of motherhood, Janet, with Johnny in tow, departs for London.

The De Mullin family is associated with decay, illness, and death. The mill—which was once the source of the De Mullin wealth—is now deteriorated. When the play opens, Mr. De Mullin is ill and we soon learn that the De Mullins have a history of bad health. And the play ends with an image of and reference to death: *"his grey head bowed on his chest,"* Mr. De Mullin repeats that he is the last of his line. Unlike Mr. De Mullin and his ancestors, Janet and her son enjoy good health. Echoing Richard Wetherby and unwittingly criticizing all the duty-bound characters in Hankin's plays, Johnny says, as his mother has taught him, that his duty is "to be healthy and to be happy." The play's Greek epigraph means, "it is best to be healthy," and so the play shows: Janet's and Johnny's healthy ways are preferable to older, unhealthy traditions.

Mr. De Mullin and Mrs. Clouston hold that a woman with "position" should never manage money; in fact, in order to retain the family reputation, she should *do* nothing except take pride in her ancestry and be dependent upon a man. Mr. De Mullin explains, "The only form of independence that is possible or desirable for a woman is that she shall be dependent upon her husband or, if she is unmarried, on her nearest male relative." Mr. De Mullin, Mrs. Clouston, and even Hester take pride in believing that *no* De Mullin has ever been in trade, and Mr. De Mullin is proud that his ancestors did nothing. By way of contrast, Janet scorns Mrs. Clouston's and Mr. De Mullin's ideals of duty, position, and propriety and advocates instead change and work: "I believe in people uprooting themselves and doing something with their lives. What was the good of the De Mullins going on living down here century after century, always a little poorer, and a little poorer, selling a farm here, mortgaging another there, instead of going out into the world to seek their fortunes? We've stayed too long in one place, we De Mullins. We shall never be worth anything sleeping away our lives down at Brendon." In *The Last of the DeMullins* work and change mean health and life; unproductivity and stasis, illness and death.

Against this code of living in the past, of doing nothing, and of depending upon men Janet rebels. She has told her son that everyone should be of "some use in the world," and she tells her father, "I owe no one obedience. I am of full age and can order my life as I please. Is a woman never to be considered old enough to manage her own affairs? Is she to go down to her grave everlastingly under tutelage? Is she always to be obeying a father when she's not obeying a husband? Well, I for one will not submit to such nonsense. I'm sick of this everlasting *obe-*

dience." Instead, Janet glories both in her work, which she compares to a child, and even more so in her own boy she has had out of wedlock. Realizing that marriage can be another form of slavery, Janet follows her self-interest and tries to realize her potential.

In Hankin's plays a woman's self-potential is best achieved in motherhood:

> These poor women who go through life listless and dull, who have never felt the joys and the pains a mother feels, how they would envy me if they knew! If they knew! To know that a child is your very own, is a part of you. That you have faced sickness and pain and death itself for it. That it is yours and nothing can take it from you because no one can understand its wants as you do. To feel its soft breath on your cheek, to soothe it when it is fretful and still it when it cries, that is motherhood and that is glorious!

Elsewhere Janet insists that a woman cannot be happy, or even keep her looks, without children. Not only does Janet glorify motherhood, but also she belittles fatherhood: "Oh come, I could have got along quite well without a father, if it comes to that. And so could Hester." Fathers are unimportant; so are husbands. Janet explains to her mother that, after her son was born, "I didn't care for anybody any more except Johnny." Janet in fact and philosophy reduces the family to child and mother.

Compared to most Victorian plays and most plays publicly produced in Edwardian London, dramas produced privately were free to treat sexual topics candidly. Accordingly, they sometimes reflect a more modern view of sexuality—for example, by showing sexual longings in both females and males—but they invariably depict illicit sexual relations as causing unhappiness, and their language and endings are virtually always decorous and conventionally moral. Thus one can understand why Hankin's play showing a happy but husbandless mother rejecting her family (especially male) ties sent shock waves into Edwardian London.

In late Victorian plays dealing with women and marriage—
Wilde's *Lady Windermere's Fan* (1892) and *A Woman of No
Importance* (1893), Pinero's *The Second Mrs. Tanqueray* (1893),
The Notorious Mrs. Ebbsmith (1895), and *The Benefit of a Doubt*
(1895), Jones's *The Case of Rebellious Susan* (1894) and *The
Masqueraders* (1894)—"the final attitudes were conservative:
sin was punished, marriage was preserved, and the double stand-
ard was treated as a natural law."[2] Unlike these popular plays
of the 1890s, *The Last of the De Mullins* reveals sin unpunished
(Janet prospers); marriage avoided (Janet is proof that sometimes
one can do well without it); and the double standard rejected
(Janet has as much independence as a man).

   Allied with and preceding Hankin in the theatrical depiction
of women as rebels against their own lot were Ibsen, Granville
Barker, and especially Shaw and Brieux.

   The subtitle to the 1909 printing of *The Last of the De Mullins*,
A Play without a Preface, hints at Shaw's influence. Hankin's
indebtedness to Shaw is perhaps best seen by comparing Janet
to Vivie Warren of Shaw's *Mrs. Warren's Profession*. Like Vivie,
Janet is iconoclastic, assertive, confident, independent, and
self-realizing. Both reject their families; both choose business
rather than a man, presumably with happy consequences. Both
could agree with Grace Tranfield in Shaw's *The Philanderer*
that "no woman is the property of a man. A woman belongs
to herself and to nobody else."[3] Janet is also Shavian in that
she is above all a mother, although unlike Shavian mothers,
Janet is unmarried.

   At least two more dramas have close and instructive similarities
to *The Last of the De Mullins*: Brieux's *The Three Daughters
of M. Dupont* and Hankin's own *The Return of the Prodigal*.

   The Last of the De Mullins might appropriately by retitled
The Two Daughters of Mr. De Mullin. In Hankin's important
yet evidently unpublished essay of the spring of 1904, "The
Propagandist as Playwright"(see Selected Bibliography), he
wrote that *The Three Daughters of M. Dupont* was probably
Brieux's masterpiece, and in March of 1905 the Stage Society

produced Hankin's translation of the play.[4] *The Last of the De Mullins* was not performed until three and one-half years after Brieux's play was staged, but the two dramas contain numerous and not entirely coincidental similarities. Compared to *The Last of the De Mullins*, Brieux's play is longer, more passionate, more sexually explicit, and more didactic, with the characters existing more as mouthpieces for their creator than as characters in their own right. Nonetheless, *The Last of the De Mullins* and *The Three Daughters of M. Dupont* have numerous parallels in characterization, plot, and theme.

Brieux's *The Three Daughters of M. Dupont* is a tidy compendium of female life-styles. Given a society where women are considered inferior to men–are considered in fact as a combination of brainless children, servants, housekeepers, and concubines–most women face the unhappy alternatives of the three daughters of M. Dupont: spinsterhood, prostitution, or degrading marriage. The two daughters of *The Last of the De Mullins* parallel the three daughters in Brieux's play. Like Hester De Mullin, Caroline Dupont is slow to forgive, is inhibited, loses the man she hopes to marry, and is likely to remain a frustrated spinster. Janet De Mullin is a composite of Angèle and Julie Dupont. Both Janet and Angèle have left home, have had an illegitimate child, and are estranged from their families. (The main difference between these two characters is that Janet runs a hat shop, whereas after Angèle's child died, Angèle became a prostitute.) Janet parallels Julie Dupont in her advocacy of women's rights; both resist the obedience demanded by men. Both also passionately defend motherhood.

Finally, *The Last of the De Mullins* has numerous similarities to Hankin's own *The Return of the Prodigal*. Both depict a prodigal returning to a home that has transformed a daughter into a spinster by not allowing her to marry beneath her station; both plays, then, depict the shaping force of environment. Each also criticizes the rigidity of dogmatic families that overvalue reputation and position. Mrs. Clouston and Mr. De Mullin are latter-day versions of Lady Faringford and Mr. Jackson:

they are all opinionated, snobbish, and patronizing. Clashing with these older characters are Eustace and Janet, who are iconoclastic, candid, undutiful, unrepentant, and avowedly selfish.

Generally speaking, though, Eustace is a carefree and cheerful failure; Janet, an earnest and didactic success. Yet Eustace's insouciance and wit make him more engaging than Janet, who often lacks detachment and humor, particularly in the last act when she's suffering from a prolonged visit with her family. It is easier to listen to and believe in Eustace than Janet, who often takes herself too seriously, frequently strains to be heard, and is severely judgmental. As is exemplified in her comments about two friends of the De Mullins, Miss Deanes and Mr. Brown, Janet sometimes sounds like Lady Faringford and Mrs. Clouston:

> JANET: What a fool Miss Deanes is!
> MRS. CLOUSTON [*indifferently*]. She always was, wasn't she?
> JANET: I suppose so. Going on in that way about a ridiculous cocatoo! And that *hideous* little curate!

Sometimes Janet seems even more intolerant than Mrs. Clouston. She lashes out at Mr. and Mrs. Bulstead, Mrs. Clouston, Mr. De Mullin, Monty Bulstead, Miss Deanes, Mr. Brown, her own sister, the plain Bulstead daughter—at virtually every character in the play except her mother and her own son.

Janet has more than the self-confidence of previous Hankin heroes; unlike them, she often takes a superior position. Her moments of sympathy with others are few, and egotism is prominent in her rebellion: "[*passionately*]. . . . Whatever happens, even if Johnny should come to hate me for what I did, I shall always be glad to have been his mother. At least I shall have lived." Previous Hankin heroes are generally imperturable, commonsensical, yet kind. Janet has many commonsensical ideas, but her anger often crushes all in its path.

The Last of the De Mullins shares a flaw with *The Three Daughters of M. Dupont:* vital characterization is sacrificed to theme.

Too often Janet is merely the author's mouthpiece. There is a further weakness in the play: missing is the subtle treatment of conflict in *The Charity that Began at Home* and *The Cassilis Engagement*. Janet is flawed, but Mr. De Mullin and Mrs. Clouston have neither a single virtue nor an appealing idea—no due to those devils.

Hankin deserves credit, though, for his insight into and sympathy for woman's plight: Janet had to lie to get a job in London *or* face near poverty as a governess or school teacher—two of the few socially acceptable jobs open to an Edwardian woman. Nonetheless, the play is scarcely revolutionary because, as Janet herself is aware, hers is an exceptional case:

> HESTER [*half laughing, half crying hysterically*]: You seem to think every woman ought to behave as shamefully as you did.
> JANET [*grimly*]: No, Hester. I don't think that. To do as I did needs pluck and brains—and five hundred pounds. Everything most women haven't got, poor things. So they must marry or remain childless.

Thus, *The Last of the De Mullins* shows that the alternatives for women remain either marriage or childless spinsterhood—*not* Janet's successful rebellion. Like Eustace, Janet only exposes her parents' and sister's situations; by the end of both *The Return of the Prodigal* and *The Last of the De Mullins* nothing substantial has changed: Violet and Hester remain trapped, while Eustace and Janet leave. Both plays show a stultifying family and their daughter-victim, rather than a solution to such conditions.

In a 1909 issue of *Punch* Hankin slyly alludes to his then recent venture and perhaps suggests he's aware of its shortcomings: "Set up the pulpit on the stage—/The dramatist secure inside it/Thumping his cushion in a rage./That is the modern mode. I tried it." As was mentioned at the beginning of this chapter, some critics viewed Hankin's new approach as his most successful, partly because of the play's affirmative philosophy and its emotional heroine. Generally, observers who complained that Hankin's earlier plays were "cynical" and without both positive philosophy and passionate characters admired *The Last of the De Mullins*. Nonetheless, it is no more affirmative than previous Hankin plays, and its heroine is less engaging than previous Hankin protagonists. The shrill tone usually submerged in Hankin's other dramas is here given rein in the facile criticism of an almost extinct feudal society. In imitating plays by Shaw and Brieux, *The Last of the De Mullins* is excessively derivative. When Hankin follows other playwrights too closely, as he does with his portrayal of the passionate and didactic Janet, he writes his least amusing, least understated, least successful play. He is far more effective in his *Three Plays with Happy Endings*, where *"Life is a comedy to those who think, a tragedy to those who feel*," where it is "the dramatist's business to represent life, not to argue about it,"[5] and where individual foibles, class pretensions, and social evils are exposed by ironic, amused, and amusing protagonists.

Notes

1. *Bernard Shaw's Letters to Granville Barker*, ed. C. B. Purdom (New York: Theatre Arts Books, 1957), pp. 142–43.

2. Samuel Hynes, *The Edwardian Turn of Mind* (Princeton: Princeton University Press, 1968), pp. 174–75.

3. Bernard Shaw, *The Philanderer*, in *The Collected Works of Bernard Shaw* (New York: Wm. H. Wise, 1930), 7: 73.

4. Eugène Brieux, *The Three Daughters of M. Dupont*, in *Three Plays by Brieux*, trans. St. John Hankin (New York: Brentano's, 1914).

5. St. John Hankin, "A Note on Happy Endings," in *The Dramatic Works of St. John Hankin*, ed. John Drinkwater (London: Martin Secker, 1912), 3: 121.

7

Last Stages:
Thompson, The Burglar Who Failed,
The Constant Lover

In Hankin's remaining months he penned three other works, a partial draft for a three-act play *Thompson*, and two one-act plays, *The Burglar Who Failed* and *The Constant Lover*.

Originally entitled by Hankin as *Thompson's Escape: A Rather Heartless Comedy*, the play was unproduced until April 1913. Its plot and characterizations closely parallel Hankin's own *The Charity that Began at Home*. In both plays an idealistic, young woman chooses as a potential mate a practical man with whom she has little in common, but in the course of events, he gives her up to his rival, a more appropriate partner, and cheerfully leaves. The main satiric target in *Thompson* is hero worship and its attendant self-delusion. *Thompson* shows no education of its heroine. By the end of the play, its hero-worshiping young lady (Helen Vaughan) decides to shift her allegiance to an earnest, heroic man (Gerald Latimer), who dazzled her by borrowing a gun from a passing territorial and shooting an escaped lion from a circus. Two years before the play's opening Helen had idolized James Thompson after she believed him eaten by sharks while rescuing women from a sinking ship. Unexpectedly, he turns up at the Vaughan's small house in Maidenhead and, sounding like other Hankin heroes, voices his skepticism about heroism, marriage, long-term plans, and work. (His name, as Harry Geduld reminded me, doubtless alludes to James Thompson, the nineteenth-century atheist-skeptic-poet.) Typically, he claims that "the fighting instinct is out of place in this police-ridden civilisation of ours. It's all very sad; but I'm afraid we've got to put up with the world as we find it." His straightforward attempts to disabuse Helen of her romantic notions merely confuse and upset her, and at the end of the play, shortly after he announces to Helen's mother that he is already engaged to Millicent Fish "of the Kentucky Fishes," he good-naturedly yields Helen to his rival/friend and leaves to return to America.

According to George Calderon's brief preface to the printed play, in the draft which Mrs. Hankin sent to him after Hankin's death, act 1 "was written out with a certain air of finality; the rest was a pretty full sketch, covering some twenty pages," and Calderon further explains that he took "full liberty in dealing with his [Hankin's] notes."[1] Since the play—including the first act—was both altered and completed by Calderon, it is erroneous to treat *Thompson* merely as Hankin's final play. In fact, it cannot be considered a Hankin play at all unless the original manuscript unexpectedly turns up, as Thompson did, and Hankin's contributions can be determined. Although the play does have some parallels to Hankin's previous works, it was altered and concluded by Calderon. As a consequence, except for a few changes which Calderon explains in his preface, it is impossible to say with certainty which parts of this play are genuine Hankin, which not, no further corroborative evidence being available. Instead of viewing *Thompson* as Hankin's final play, it should be considered a Calderon creation lacking Hankin's sureness of style and deft humor.

Virtually every critic of the one-act *The Burglar Who Failed* has pointed out its similarities to act 1 of Shaw's earlier *Arms and the Man*, and rightly so since both acts show a man of experience under improbable and amusing circumstances trying to educate an innocent young lady. (This attempted education is a frequent theme in Shaw, appearing even in his first novel, *Immaturity*.) Nonetheless, the play is scarcely didactic. Like such Shavian farces as *How He Lied to Her Husband* and *The Admirable Bashville, The Burglar Who Failed* contains improbable actions and broad characterizations primarily for amusement.

When produced at the Criterion Theatre in October of 1908, the play was Hankin's first to be staged in a commercial theater. *The Burglar Who Failed* includes Dolly Maxwell, a self-reliant, athletic young lady; her staid mother, Mrs. Maxwell; and William Simpkins, whose professional name is Bill Bludgeon, a former footman discharged for drunkenness. The action begins at about 10:00 P.M. in Dolly's bedroom in the Maxwell house in Wimbledon. Mrs. Maxwell warns her daughter about a thief who has recently been active in the neighborhood, then says good night. The malefactor is soon discovered—when he drops his jimmy, then falls to sneezing because he has caught a cold in the draft under the bed. While he is still under the bed, Dolly disarms the intruder with some adroit hockey-stick play:

> DOLLY You wicked ruffian! [*Hits his hand sharply with stick. He drops revolver. With dexterous sweep of hockey stick she sweeps it over to herself, picks it up, cocks it and levels it at his head.*] If you move another inch I'll fire.
>
> BLUDGEON [*in terror, entire change of tone. Gruff menace turned to shrill note of alarm*]: Look out! You've cocked it! It'll go off if you're not careful. It's loaded. [*Backing ignominiously.*]

Shortly thereafter, the thief takes off his false hair, false beard, and false nose *"and sits revealed as a seedy, pallid little pug-nosed person of the meekest type."* In the amusing discussion that follows, Hankin reveals the occupational hazards of thievery. After the burglar admits he's a failure as a thief and decides to change professions, Dolly promises to help him secure a new position. Mrs. Maxwell momentarily returns to Dolly's room and the burglar just escapes detection by hiding in Dolly's wardrobe cupboard, then Dolly helps him escape into the night—although he leaves behind his revolver.

Dolly shares with the Shavian female vitality, self-reliance, and poise; both also intimidate a man, then treat him as if he were a child. As in his own previous plays, Hankin matches this rebellious young character with a self-serious, worrisome, duty-demanding older woman, in this case Dolly's mother, whom Dolly manages with genial humor.

More of the play, however, is devoted to the discussion between Dolly and the burglar, and we, along with Dolly, learn that the trade is nerve-wracking, unrewarding, and dangerous:

> BLUDGEON: Since then [the time one of his intended victims ran at Bludgeon brandishing a large stick] I've carried a revolver, just in self-defence. I needed it, too, a week later.
>
> DOLLY [*horrified*]: Did you kill somebody with it?
>
> BLUDGEON: Not a man, miss. Only a dog.
>
> DOLLY [*sternly*]: So you shot Binky!
>
> BLUDGEON: Was that his name, miss? A great bull-dog up at Miss Mallaby's.
>
> DOLLY [*indignantly*]: I think it was horrid of you to shoot Binky. It was cowardly.
>
> BLUDGEON: Cowardly! Bravest deed I ever done, miss, by a long chalk. It takes nerve to shoot a bull-dog, I can tell you, when he's got his teeth in your leg. You'll very likely shoot your own leg if you're not careful.
>
> DOLLY: Had he his teeth in your leg? I remember they said his mouth was full of blood when they found him.
>
> BLUDGEON: It was. My blood!
>
> DOLLY: Still I don't think you ought to have shot him. He was such a friendly doggie with people he knew.
>
> BLUDGEON: Then he evidently didn't know me, miss. I tried to make friends with him. I said "Good dog" and "Down, sir," and all the things one does say to a dog one wants to be friendly with, but he wouldn't pay any attention. He just growled and came at me. I simply had to shoot. And, of course, that spoilt my game at the Mallabys', for the noise woke everybody. Old Mrs. Mallaby threw up her window and screamed fit to wake the dead, and I had to run for it.

In addition to exposing the burglar's activities, Hankin touches upon a practical cure for such social problems. Instead of having the burglar turned over to the police, Hankin, as Shaw might well have done, has Dolly offer him a job. Perhaps Hankin was influenced by a passage in act 2 of Shaw's *Captain Brassbound's Conversion* (1899) in which Lady Cicely recounts how she and Sir Howard

> caught a burglar one night at Waynflete when he [Sir How-ard] was staying with us; and I insisted on his locking the poor man up, until the police came, in a room with a window opening on the lawn. The man came back next day and said he must return to a life of crime unless I gave him a job in the garden; and I did. It was much more sensible than giving him ten years penal servitude.[2]

Whether or not Hankin was influenced by this passage, both in its farcical characterization and action and in its practical solution to a social problem, *The Burglar Who Failed* is Hankin's most Shavian play.

Not that Hankin can be said to develop the play's themes. The work is primarily for amusement, not amusement *and* enlightenment, and Dolly and Bill are a bit too eccentric to be seen as people. For the only time in his career, Hankin wrote a play that stresses amusing, surprising situations, *not* an unorthodox, thoughtful, and thought-provoking protagonist. *The Burglar Who Failed* is a limited success, quite amusing but derivative and without the overtones of Hankin's best work.

In Hankin's suicide note to his wife in June of 1909, he alluded to his final completed play: " 'Think of me as the constant lover' "[3] Thus, even on the brink of death Hankin displayed his distinctive and typical blend of the comic and tragic. A few months earlier Hankin had evidently also referred to *The Constant Lover* in an interview: "I have a one-act masterpiece done, but I don't see who is to produce it. It wants very careful casting and it is not very well suited for the rough-and-tumble work of playing

the stalls into their seats."[4] Although the play was not produced
until January of 1912, Hankin's judgment of it as a masterpiece is another tribute to his acumen.

The plot of *The Constant Lover: A Comedy of Youth in One Act*
is slight. Typical of Hankin's dramas, the play stresses characterization and ideas while repeating the successful minimal
action of *The Return of the Prodigal*, *The Charity that Began
at Home*, and, to a lesser extent, *The Two Mr. Wetherbys*: a non-
conformist outsider confronts the duty-stricken, amuses the
audience/reader as he outrages but does not change the conventional character(s), and then resumes his own independent
way of life. In *The Constant Lover* Evelyn Rivers, eighteen or
twenty, meets Cecil Harburton, twenty-five, as she has now
every afternoon since their initial meeting a week earlier. The
two talk, revealing their mutual attraction but dissimilar out-
looks. At length Evelyn is so shocked by Cecil's irreverent ideas
that she resists his charms and leaves, by inference to return to
Reggie Townsend, a dutiful but insipid boyfriend.

Virtually every critic of the play has discussed its sunny,
high-spirited qualities. From the opening curtain, which reveals
a bright glade full of chirping birds and a protagonist wearing
"a straw hat and the lightest of grey flannel suits," this cheerful
mood is sustained. Typical is the exchange between Cecil and
Evelyn that accounts for the play's title:

> EVELYN: . . . Reggie is quite different from you. Reggie's
> love is true and constant . . .
> CECIL: Well, I'm a *constant* lover if you come to that.
> EVELYN: You aren't. You know you aren't.
> CECIL: Yes I am. A constant lover is a lover who is con-
> stantly in love.
> EVELYN: Only with the same person.
> CECIL: It doesn't say so. It only says constant.

The mood and setting of the play mellow our response to Cecil
and his ideas:

Hankin has been at some pains to establish the mood of a summer idyll in this play, and his choice of *milieu* casts a mellow glow over the ideas and attitudes of the hero. Cecil Harburton is actually as tough-minded and unconventional as his predecessors, but the very fact that his ideas are expressed in images and symbols from the bright summer world about him lends them a peculiar charm. It is the essence of the comedy in *The Constant Lover* that the familiar machinery of "poetic" and sentimental romance is put to anti-romantic and unsentimental uses.[5]

The play sustains this mellow tone by emphasizing relaxation, the beauty of nature, and the joys of unmarried love.

As the play progresses, however, a darker seam appears, beginning with the bitter tone of Cecil's explanation to Evelyn that various sorts of birds "spend their whole lives building nests and laying eggs and hatching them. And when the chickens come out the father has to fuss round finding worms. And the nest's abominably overcrowded and the babies are perpetually squalling, and that drives the husband to the public-house, and it's all as uncomfortable as the Devil—."Like Eustace Jackson's cheerfulness, Cecil's equanimity is momentarily threatened by both an awareness of life's frequent degrading conditions and an anger and pride, which imply that he is not entirely detached and in control of himself. Later, this somber undercurrent is more evident when Cecil exhorts Evelyn:

Let's be in love while we can. Youth is the time to be in love, isn't it? Soon you and I will be dull and stupid and middle-aged like all the other tedious people. And then it will be too late. Youth passes so quickly. Don't let's waste a second of it. They say the May-fly only lives for one day. He is born in the morning. All the afternoon he flutters over the river in the sunshine, dodging the trout and flirting with other May-flies. And at evening he dies. Think of the poor May-fly who happens to be born on a wet day! The tragedy of it!

This passage is striking both because of its vivid, complex image—rare in Hankin's writings—and because this view of life's cruelty, fragility, competitiveness, uncertainty, inconsequence, and brevity is not from *The Return of the Prodigal*, but from *The Constant Lover* complete with its cheerful, sunny May setting. Even in this passage, however, Hankin once again displays both his usual light touch—the May-fly fluttering in the sunshine and "flirting"—and the tragic overtones indicated above. The play's epigraph *"As of old when the world's heart was lighter,"* likewise hints of the play's underlying melancholy strain. When Hankin wrote *The Constant Lover* he was approaching his fortieth birthday—in itself a traumatic event for many people—and his already weak health was failing. Hankin had had surgery in 1908, and the epigraph and subject of *The Last of the De Mullins* both suggest a preoccupation with health. Perhaps the melancholy moments in *The Constant Lover* reflect Hankin's awareness of the passing of youth and vitality.

Like Hankin's previous dramas, *The Constant Lover* exposes earnest, dutiful, industrious behavior, here represented by Evelyn, her cousin/boyfriend Reggie, and her parents. After Cecil tells Evelyn that he loves her, then calmly admits that he has been in love many times before, Hankin satirizes several Victorian bromides:

> EVELYN [*struggling for words*]: Do you mean to say you've been in love with girls before? *Other* girls?
> CECIL [*apparently genuinely astonished at the question*]: Of course I have.
> EVELYN: And been engaged to them?
> CECIL: Not engaged. I've never been engaged so far. But I've been in love over and over again. [EVELYN *stamps her foot with rage—turning away from him.*] My dear girl, what *is* the matter? You look quite cross. [*Rises.*]
> EVELYN [*furious*]: And you're not even *ashamed* of it?
> CECIL [*roused to sit up by this question*]: Ashamed of it? Ashamed of being in love? How can you say such a thing! Of course I'm not ashamed. What's the good of being alive at all if one isn't to be in love? I'm perpetually in love. In

fact, I'm hardly ever out of love—with somebody.

EVELYN [*still furious*]: Then if you're in love, why don't you get engaged? A man has no business to make love to [court] a girl and not be engaged to her. It's not right.

CECIL [*reasoning with her*]: That's the parents' fault. I told you parents were preposterous people. They won't allow me to get engaged.

EVELYN: Why not?

CECIL: Oh, for different reasons. They say I'm not *serious* enough. Or that I don't work enough. Or that I haven't got enough money. Or else they simply say they "don't think I'm fitted to make their daughter happy."

Again, as in so many scenes in Hankin's drama, the protagonist clashes with the staid and conventional.

To those who know Hankin's other plays, Cecil is cut from the same cloth as Richard Wetherby, Eustace Jackson, and Hugh Verreker. With Richard Wetherby, Cecil shares a gusto for life in its simple, sensuous pleasures; Cecil is a less angry, more affectionate Eustace, similarly contrasted with a money-making rival. And both Cecil and Hugh Verreker caution against romantic notions of marriage. In common with his predecessors, Cecil rejects the Victorian ideals of work and sacrifice: "To sit in a frowsy office adding up figures when the sky's blue and the weather's heavenly, *that's* wasting time. The only real way in which one can waste time is not to enjoy it, to spend one's day blinking at a ledger and never notice how beautiful the world is, and how good it is to be alive. To be only making money when one might be making love, *that* is wasting time!" In the best Hankin manner Cecil displays candor, spontaneity, perceptiveness, independence, joyfulness.

Even though Cecil shares many qualities with previous Hankin protagonists, he has greater emotional capacity. For instance, although Richard Wetherby, Eustace Jackson, and Hugh Verreker occasionally show concern, Cecil often displays kindness: "*Much concerned,*" "*Takes her handkerchief and . . .* [dries her tears] *tenderly,*" (see fig. 4) and later when Evélyn becomes distraught

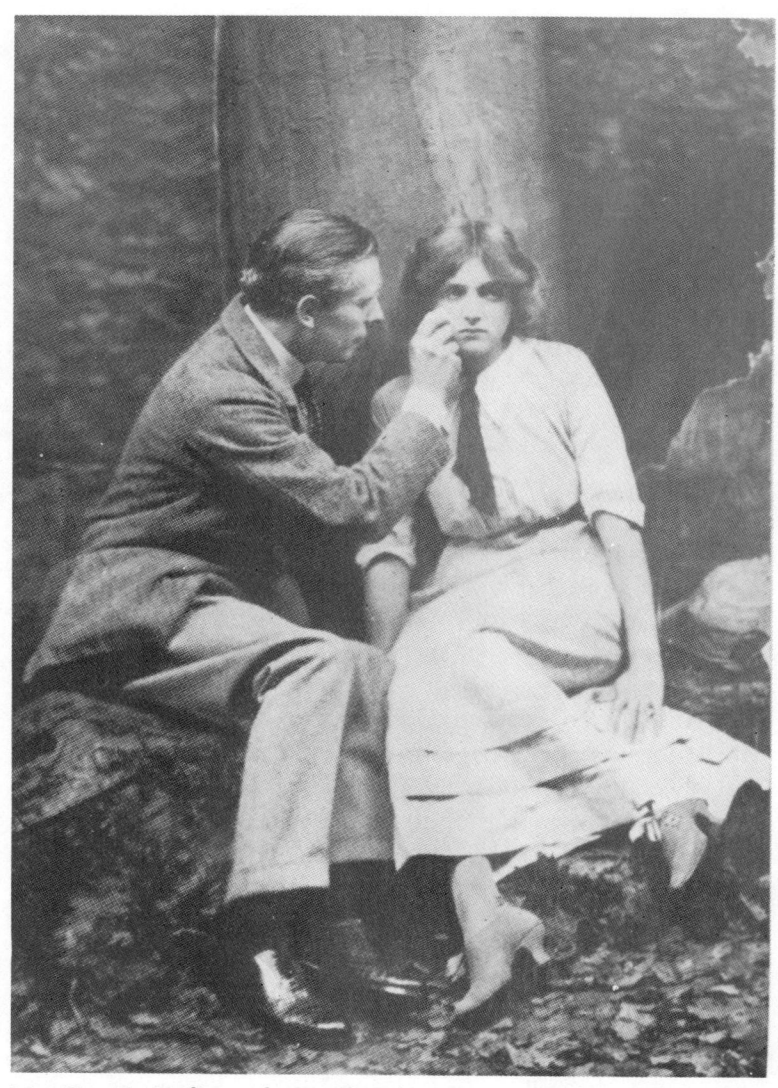

Mr. Dennis Eadie and Miss Gladys Cooper in the Original Production of *The Constant Lover.*

by Cecil's philosophy, he is *"genuinely distressed,"* and he *"Lays hand on her shoulder."* Finally, when Evelyn leaves, *"*CECIL *watches her departure with a smile, half amused, half pained, till she is long out of sight. Then with half a sigh he turns back to his tree.]* CECIL *[reseating himself]*: Poor Reggie! *[Reopens his book and settles himself to read again. A cuckoo hoots loudly from a distant thicket and is answered by another.* CECIL *looks up from his book to listen as the curtain falls.].*" Less often than previous Hankin protagonists does Cecil evade a painful issue with a joke. And for the first time in a Hankin play, the protagonist is left alone at play's end.

After imitating other playwrights in *The Last of the De Mullins* and *The Burglar Who Failed,* Hankin returned to an earlier approach and perfected it. Largely through the vehicle of Cecil's character, *The Constant Lover* displays a compendium of Hankin's themes. That Hankin managed to satirize the sacred cows of earnestness, duty, work, and marriage, while suggesting the probable meaninglessness of human endeavors and the desirability of fleeting natural pleasures attests to the thematic richness of this compact play. Because *The Constant Lover* handles these themes in a provocative and persuasive manner and its characterizations in an amusing and engaging fashion, the play is, as Hankin had told an interviewer, "a one-act masterpiece."

Notes

1. *The Plays of St. John Hankin,* ed. John Drinkwater (London: Martin Secker, 1923), 2: 221.

2. Bernard Shaw, *Captain Brassbound's Conversion,* in *The Collected Works of Bernard Shaw* (New York: Wm. H. Wise, 1930), 9: 260.

3. "Dramatic Suicide at Llandrindod Wells," *Radnorshire Standard,* 26 June 1909, p. 10, col. 1. Also quoted in numerous other Hankin obituaries.

4. "In the Days of my Youth," *M.A.P.* 22 (10 April 1909): 349. This interview is reprinted in Appendix B.

5. John Drew O'Neill, "The Comedy of St. John Hankin" (Ph.D. diss., University of Michigan, 1954), pp. 299–300.

8

Epilogue

From 1903 to 1909 the Edwardian Mephistopheles didn't simply write plays and continue to be a frequent contributor to *Punch* (see Selected Bibliography). During this period he helped run the Stage Society and published his five full-length plays, drama reviews in *The Academy*, and major essays about Shaw, the plays of Oscar Wilde, a London art theater, an endowed theater for London, and the movement to abolish censorship of plays.

In his writing from 1903 to 1909 Hankin repeatedly criticized the theater of his time. Such established individuals as actor-manager Beerbohm Tree, critic William Archer, and playwright Arthur Wing Pinero were frequent topics. Also targets were unnamed playwrights, critics and the censor. Hankin often faulted so-called serious plays marred by improbable characters, incidents, and endings, since, as he frequently wrote, the best drama accurately reflects life. He also chided critics for not supporting plays with ideas,[1] and in his unpublished essay on Brieux wrote that serious drama need not inevitably be excluded from the commercial stage. Hankin also thought that censorship was a cause of the shortcomings of Edwardian theater and often said so: "How can you expect to have a national drama of serious intellectual interest if you cut it off from all the most vital and inspiring subjects."[2]

In a speech at an annual dinner for the Stage Society in 1906 (reprinted in Appendix B), Hankin suggested that the British populace in encouraging actors and actor-managers at the expense of writers was partly to blame for the state of British drama:

> The orthodox British attitude towards the Drama is to recognize everybody connected with it except the dramatist. That is just what the Stage Society has done. "The Players," "The Critics," are duly honoured. The Dramatist is ignored. That is the universal practice in England. You can observe it, if you will, on the hoardings on which theatrical events appear. There you find the name of the theatre in large type, the name of the play in larger type, the name of the actor or actress in very, very large type; and if it is a theatre that is so fortunate as to possess an actor-manager, his name appears in enormous type. The name of the author is either hidden away in some corner, or not given at all. . . . I may add that I am informed that 90 per cent. of the playgoers of London believe that "Nero" was *written* by Mr. Beerbohm Tree, and as the artist requires the stimulus of applause to do his best work, the inevitable result is that in England we often get admirable acting but poor drama.[3]

According to Hankin, the British also failed to read plays; they bought novels and thus supported novelists, but unlike Europeans, Edwardians bought and read few dramas.[4]

Given such conditions, it's unsurprising that Hankin wrote in 1907 that the Edwardian theater was static:

> Politics, sociology, literature, Fine Arts, [*sic*] have moved in England during the past fifteen years. New ideas have come in, old ideas have gone out. The English theatre has not moved at all. . . . The Court Theatre has just given a few tentative matinees of *Hedda Gabler*. Miss Robins was doing the same fifteen years ago. At the St. James's Mr. Pinero has replaced *Mrs. Tanqueray* with *His House in Order*—not exactly progress. The Stage Society is merely the Independent Theatre in a new incarnation. Musical comedy [which Hankin elsewhere described as "merely another name for a display of pretty young ladies in a decent minimum of pretty cloth-

ing"] is still the mainstay of our most successful managements.
Plus ça change plus c'est la même chose.[5]

Hankin's own drama, however, is not so progressive as his
criticism. Both his stage techniques, such as quieting a full
room so that an intimate dialogue can take place, and many
of his characters are conventional. His themes, protagonists, and
endings, however, are more novel and more in line with his
criticism. All of his plays challenge commonplace ideas by means
of surprising, provocative protagonists: a happy, separated
husband (Richard Wetherby); a blackmailing prodigal (Eustace
Jackson); a disreputable yet kind guest (Hugh Verreker); a
loving, scheming mother (Mrs. Cassilis); a happily unwed,
working mother (Janet De Mullin); a timid burglar (Bill Bludgeon); and an irreverent bachelor constantly in love (Cecil Harburton). "It was St. John Hankin's aim as a dramatist to show his
contemporaries the other side of the picture . . . each [of his major
characters] taking openly the side that was not at the time usually
taken openly, however often it was taken in secret."[6] By basing
the endings of his plays upon the characters, not conventions or
audience expectations, Hankin was also innovative.

Hankin's plays have uncomplicated plots, whose few actions
are usually determined by their commonsensical protagonists.
Thus, for example, in *The Return of the Prodigal* Eustace returns
home and, true to his character, blackmails his family and leaves.
By way of contrast,

> the old-fashioned playwright set out to act on your nerves,
> to give you a surprise or a shock, to lead up to an exciting
> situation (the *scène à faire*), to make you weep or creep. To
> do this he was prepared to sacrifice probability, possibility
> even. To him character-drawing was nothing, situation
> everything. . . . Holding the mirror up to nature came second
> to him—if it came at all. With the Tchekoff school char-
> acter-drawing and the truthful delineation of life as it actually
> is come first.[7]

What Hankin says here often applies as well to his own drama, especially after his first play. Like Chekhov, Zola, Granville Barker, and other playwrights of the independent theater movement, Hankin largely rejected the well-made play that dominated nineteenth-century drama and advocated instead the modern drama of lifelike theme and character.

Thus, less traditional protagonists populate Hankin's drama. His heroes—Richard Wetherby, Eustace Jackson, Hugh Verreker, and Cecil Harburton—suggest both in word and deed that the individual should neither take himself too seriously nor slavishly follow convention and thus miss life's pleasures. Usually his male protagonists clash with characters who are older, wealthy, reputable, yet incapable of pleasure, self-realization, or kindness. Hankin's hero is also confident, charming, and candid. Occasionally, he uses his wit to avoid sentiment. Furthermore, he has a quick and incisive mind. The children of Hankin's brain are, like Shaw's main characters, vital creations that think and talk in an intelligent yet entertaining way. Usually, Hankin's hero neither righteously and indignantly judges follies and evils, nor expects to banish them. Instead, he tries to be a cheerful, amused observer of both the world and himself. Yet in Hankin's plays runs a contrary strain, and occasional angry outbursts, especially in *The Return of the Prodigal*, suggest that he could maintain an amused perspective only with difficulty.

The Hankin heroine—made up from Mrs. Cassilis, Janet De Mullin, and Dolly Maxwell—has in common with the Hankin hero poise, selfishness, intelligence, and resourcefulness, but, unlike Hankin's heroes, she lacks amused detachment. Above all else, Mrs. Cassilis and Janet De Mullin are devoted mothers. Hankin's writings suggest a Victorian dual view: man should be an amused, commonsensical hedonist; woman, a devoted, passionate mother.

Hankin's plays attack some of the traditional targets of comedy: idealists, romantics, hypocrites, and prigs. In his plays Hankin also satirized the professions of medicine and divinity, certain kinds of charity, the advocates of duty and status quo, and their victims. In nearly all his plays Hankin shows that marriage should be based upon mutual tastes and mutual interests and that reason, rather than passion, should usually guide conduct. Hankin implied that one should question previously held beliefs, remain amused by man's follies, and live not by rigid rules but for life's simple pleasures.

None of the above themes is unusual in comedy. But one of Hankin's views sometimes jars with his usual genial tone: one can do nothing to change one's character and situation since both are dictated by heredity and environment. In this respect, Hankin was akin to literary naturalists, a similarity Harry M. Geduld first brought to my attention. Whether Hankin derived this outlook from Darwin, Zola, his own experiences—such as his contraction of malaria and the nervous breakdown of his father—or a combination of these and other sources is difficult to determine. Hankin may have been influenced by a naturalistic outlook and incorporated some of it into his comedy of manners. But it is misleading to label him a naturalist. Heredity and environment are not prominent subjects in his plays, except for *The Return of the Prodigal*. Labeling Hankin a naturalist also conjures up too many inappropriate images: man's animal instincts and appetites, especially the sexual ones, and lower-class settings and characters. A curious feature of Edwardian drama is that its most socially conscious playwrights—Shaw, Galsworthy, Barker, and, to a lesser extent, Hankin—are all middle-class dramatists who, unlike their continental naturalistic counterparts, are largely unconcerned with the problems of the working class.

In *The Two Mr. Wetherbys* Hankin had not yet found his own voice and with its inconsistent and farcical ending crippled the play's intellectual drive. *The Cassilis Engagement* is marred by too many lifeless characters. In *The Last of the De Mullins*, Hankin tried to write in the vein of Brieux and Shaw. And in *The Burglar Who Failed* Hankin produced a pale carbon copy of Shaw's plays. When Hankin was more self-reliant in *The Return of the Prodigal, The Charity that Began at Home*, and *The*

Constant Lover, he was at his best. In these plays Hankin's protagonists are engaging, provocative, and closely observed; his
plots are uncompromised; his themes ambitious yet persuasive;
and his satire effective and humorous.

Yet many critics have dismissed Hankin as merely a cynic.[8]
In "The Criminal," *The Return of the Prodigal*, and "A Man of
Impulse," Hankin is most open to the charge. As his plays reveal,
he was aware that people tend to follow their self-interests and
to hide that fact from others; in this sense of the term, Hankin
was cynical, perhaps particularly to many Victorians. However,
in the broader sense of the term – the condition of being without
affirmative values – Hankin was scarcely a cynic. In fact, in
common with other satirists, he was an entertaining although
occasionally embittered moralist, and his ethics were usually
skillfully camouflaged. Like many comedic writers, Hankin
distrusted both unthinking conventionality and foolish behavior,
yet Richard Wetherby, Eustace Jackson, Hugh Verreker, Mrs.
Cassilis, Janet De Mullin, and Cecil Harburton are hardly mis-
anthropic creations. If not always praiseworthy, they are generally
incisive, witty, life loving, and on occasion generous and kind.
All of them are proof that life can be pleasurable, even if without
underlying meaning.

Hankin's importance as a dramatist has been overlooked
by other critics understandably awed by the work of a frequent
Hankin defender, George Bernard Shaw. Of the dramatists
of his time, Hankin was most akin to Shaw, and his influence
is often evident in Hankin's plays. In deriding self-sacrifice
and satirizing idealists, Hankin was in the Shavian tradition.
In rejecting outdated codes of conduct and in insisting that
behavior be based upon its effects for the individual, Hankin
was also like Shaw. Finally, in employing iconoclastic protagonists to achieve these ends and in his faith in reason as a guide
to conduct Hankin was again like Shaw.

Nonetheless, Hankin was no docile Shavian imitator. "The
breadth of imagination, the excess and enthusiasm of Shaw
can be breath-taking and stimulating. His optimism can be

persuasive and deceiving. Hankin, however, was neither persuaded nor deceived; consequently he never tried to pitch his
comedy at the exalted level where Shaw was so at home."[9] There
are other differences between the two playwrights. Accepting
the views of Lamarck, Shaw saw evolutionary change as brought
about by Will, whereas Hankin adapted Darwinian thought
with its emphasis on heredity and environment. Furthermore,
Hankin's plays, unlike Shaw's, have little didacticism, no talk
of social reform, no talk of a Superman. Shaw and Hankin ex-
hibit two poles of thought: faith in change and resignation
to the world as it is. Frequently, Hankin's non-Shavian concern
was with the individual finding pleasure away from a repressive
society that he cannot hope to change.

Hankin's was a distinctive voice in Edwardian theater. Compared with other plays of his time, Hankin's comedies are less
geared to popular tastes, values and expectations than the
drama of J. M. Barrie, Somerset Maugham, A. W. Pinero, and
H. A. Jones—the latter two, the British avant-garde in the 1890s
still prominent during the Edwardian period. Hankin's drama
is also less optimistic than the plays of his fellow middle-class
colleagues, Shaw, Galsworthy, and Barker. And Hankin's work
is less didactic and less reformist than the drama of Shaw, Brieux,
and Caine. Generally, Hankin treated social behavior and conventions, not with the solemnity, didacticism, and melodrama
of so many of his contemporaries, but with common sense
and wit.

Although such critics as Max Beerbohm admired much of
Hankin's work, in Hankin's lifetime he had limited success
with the London stage. But most of his plays thrived for about
twenty years in the repertory theaters in the provinces. Probably
this success resulted in the 1912 and 1923 editions of Hankin's
plays. After 1923, however, interest in Hankin waned. Such
neglect is a pity. Three Hankin plays—*The Return of the Prodigal*,
The Charity That Began at Home, and *The Constant Lover*—are
worthy of revival; at least these plays stage well in my mind's
eye. (The 1973 London revival of *The Return of the Prodigal*

gives me hope in my judgment: that production received favorable reviews.) And many of Hankin's writings are of more than historical importance, more than reflections of the events and the drama of his time. Hankin's best work displays lucidity, judiciousness, and an original yet entertaining way of looking at traditional ideas and situations. In industrial, urban societies that exhalt work, materialism, and conformity, Hankin's ideas and his relaxed, iconoclastic protagonists make appealing—perhaps even healthy—reading and viewing.

Notes

1. "Mr. Bernard Shaw as Critic," in *The Dramatic Works of St. John Hankin*, ed. John Drinkwater (London: Martin Secker, 1912), 3: 167.

2. St. John Hankin, "Puritanism and the English Stage," in *The Dramatic Works of St. John Hankin*, ed. John Drinkwater (London: Martin Secker, 1912), 3: 138.

3. *Stage Society News*, no. 20 (24 March 1906), p. 73. For a photocopy of this very rare issue I am grateful to Dan H. Laurence.

4. "In the Days of my Youth," *M.A.P.* 22 (10 April 1909): 348. This interview is reprinted in Appendix B.

5. Hankin, "Mr. Bernard Shaw as Critic," pp. 156–57.

6. "Globe Theatre," *Times* (London), 25 November 1948, p. 7, col. 4.

7. St. John Hankin, "The Stage Society—The 'Moscow School' of Drama," *Academy* 72 (15 June 1907): 585.

8. "Hankin," *The Oxford Companion to the Theatre*, ed. Phyllis Hartnoll, 3d ed. (London: Oxford University Press, 1967), p. 427; W. L. Courtney, "Realistic Drama," *Old Saws and Modern Instances* (New York: E. P. Dutton, 1918), pp. 215–16; Ernest Reynolds, *Modern English Drama* (London: George G. Harrap, 1949), p. 145; A[rthur] E[ustace] Morgan, "Hankin," *Tendencies of Modern English Drama* (New York: Charles Scribner's Sons, 1924), p. 111.

9. John Drew O'Neill, "The Comedy of St. John Hankin" (Ph.D. diss., University of Michigan 1954), p. 336.

Appendix A
A Chronology

1869

25 September: Born, Southampton

1883

January: Matriculated at Malvern Public School, Worcester

1886

October: Matriculated at Merton College, Oxford

1890

Completed education at Oxford

Worked as a private tutor

Began journalistic career in London

Began writing for the *Saturday Review* (London)

1892

Elected to membership in the Savile Club (London)

1893

June: *Andrew Paterson* produced

July: *Andrew Paterson* published

July: Essay, "The Criminal," published

1894

Worked for the *Indian Daily News* (Calcutta)

Contracted malaria

December: Published a book review in the *Academy* (London)

1895

Hankin's first publication in the *Times*

1897

August: Began to review plays for the *Times*

1898

February: Essay, "The True Sublime of Boating," published

June: Began to publish in *Punch*

1899

December: Stopped reviewing plays for the *Times*

1901

Mr. Punch's Dramatic Sequels published

1 June: Married Florence Routledge in Surrey

1902

From at least this early until his death, served on the Council
of Management for the Stage Society

1903

March: *The Two Mr. Wetherbys* first produced

1904

Lost Masterpieces and Other Verses published

1905

Retired to Campden, Gloucestershire

March: Stage Society Production of Brieux's *The Three Daughters of M. Dupont*, Translated by St. John Hankin

September: *The Return of the Prodigal* first produced

1906

August: *The Two Mr. Wetherbys* produced in New York City

October: *The Charity that Began at Home* first produced

The Charity that Began at Home published

1907

The Two Mr. Wetherbys, The Return of the Prodigal, and *Three Plays with Happy Endings* all published

Health failing

February: *The Cassilis Engagement* first produced

April: *The Return of the Prodigal* revived at the Court Theatre

June: Essay, "Mr. Bernard Shaw as Critic," published

November: Essay, "How to Run an Art Theatre for London,"
published

1908

Surgery

February: Essay, "The Censorship of Plays," published

March: Letter to the *Times* from Cannes

1 May: Essay, "The Collected Plays of Oscar Wilde," published

11 May: *The Return of the Prodigal* revived by Miss Horniman at the Gaiety Theatre, Manchester

October: *The Burglar Who Failed* first produced

November: *The Charity that Began at Home* revived at the Gaiety Theatre in Manchester

1 December: Essay, "The Need for an Endowed Theatre," published

6 December: *The Last of the De Mullins* first produced

28 December: Made out his will

1909

January: Autobiographical "The Modern Dramatist to His Muse," Hankin's last publication in *Punch*

March: *The Return of the Prodigal* revived at the Gaiety Theatre in Manchester

April: Hankin interview in *M.A.P.* published

May: *The Last of the De Mullins* published

June: Short story, "A Man of Impulse," published

15 June: Died, Llandrindod Wells, Wales

Appendix B
A Speech by Hankin (1906)
And an Interview with Him (1909)

Speech at the Annual Dinner for the Stage Society in 1906 *

Mr. St. John Hankin: My Lord, Ladies, and Gentlemen, before I come to the subject of the toast I have the honour to propose—viz., the toast of the Players—I should like to say one word about Gogol. I observed that when our Chairman, in deprecating the production of Gogol's very amusing farce—which Mr. Shaw has described as "the Charley's Aunt of Russia"—told you that instead we had given you Ibsen's "Lady Inger," a groan went round this large assembly. I hope this means that I shall have the support of the greater number of those present in my strenuous efforts to get Gogol's play produced. Gogol, as you know, is one of the very greatest of Russian authors, and his play "The Inspector-General" is an extremely amusing play. It is true it is a farce, but a farce sixty years old is a classic; and I think if we accept some of Shakespeare's comedies, which are practically farces, as great literature, we may fairly accept Gogol's play at that valuation. As a play it has held the stage in Russia for sixty years, and I think it would be interesting to see it produced by the Stage Society. I hope, therefore, those who would like an amusing evening—for a change—will kindly, when they get home to-night, write to the Council, insisting that Gogol's name shall figure in the programme of the Society this season.

I now turn to my task, that of proposing "The Players." It is a great honour—but it is also onerous. The Stage Society

*From *The Stage Society News*, no. 20 (24 March 1906), pp. 73–74.

is not generally supposed to be an orthodox institution, but I notice from the toast list that in our attitude towards the Drama we are strikingly orthodox. The orthodox British attitude towards the Drama is to recognise everybody connected with it except the dramatist. That is just what the Stage Society has done. "The Players," "The Critics," are duly honoured. The Dramatist is ignored. That is the universal practice in England. You can observe it, if you will, on the hoardings on which theatrical events appear. There you find the name of the theatre in large type, the name of the play in larger type, the name of the actor or actress in very, very large type; and if it is a theatre that is so fortunate as to possess an actor-manager, his name appears in enormous type. The name of the author is either hidden away in some corner, or not given at all. If you want a crucial instance of this, I will point out to you that our Chairman has not yet learnt how Mr. Pinero pronounces his name. I may add that I am informed that 90 per cent. of the playgoers of London believe that "Nero" was *written* by Mr. Beerbohm Tree, and as the artist requires the stimulus of applause to do his best work, the inevitable result is that in England we often get admirable acting but poor drama. I have heard this remarked even of the productions of the Stage Society! Fortunately, I am here to eulogise the actors, not the dramatists. So this does not disturb me. I know that sometimes the view of our Chairman has met with some support, that the Stage Society plays are not always of the very highest order of merit. But no one has ever ventured to say that the standard of acting has been anything but the highest. The zeal, intelligence, and enthusiasm which are the note of our performances are recognised by the Press and by our members. They excite, I believe, not only admiration, but a certain amount of annoyance in the ordinary theatres which cannot make out how it is the Stage Society manages to get such admirable performances. I hope the reason is partly because we are what is called a "good audience." But I think it is also partly because we try to choose plays which, whether great or not, yet, through having real relation to life,

and not being merely conventional hack-work, give opportunities
for the artist who takes his art seriously and desires to enter
into his part to do work which is really of a high order. To single
out special names would be invidious where thanks are owed
to all, and I am sure your memories will at once supply scores
of instances of brilliant performances. If it is asked how such
acting is got, I will point out that we owe it partly to the character of the plays we produce, partly to our having no actor-manager demanding all the limelight and bent on all the good lines.
It must be very depressing for the great majority of the cast
to see that when the actor-manager is on the stage, all the light
follows him round it. It must be so damping to the players
in the dark. While I am giving this toast, I wish to lay special
stress on the work of the Producers as a branch of the profession
to which we are specially indebted. The Producer is very apt
not to get his full share of the credit of a performance, so I wish
to specially emphasise our debt to him. Some of you may have
noticed that the name of the Producer is always put in the most
conspicuous place in our programmes, in order that it may
be known who is the person behind the scenes who is bearing
so much of the burden and is largely responsible for the general
effect, the coherence, the *ensemble*. You may, some of you, ask,
"What is a Producer?" Well, a Producer, as his name implies,
has the whole control of the production. He drills the actors,
he sees that the full effect is got out of the lines and the situations,
he sees that the various characters are in due subordination
to the main theme, that the scenery is suitable—and that it
is *there*. I may tell you that scenery, like play-goers, is apt to
be late. He sees to the lighting of the scenes and their furnishing.
There is no detail too small for his attention. Last of all, and
perhaps most important, he keeps the cast in good temper,
and keeps them from bullying the author. That position is
not always a sinecure. I would ask you, therefore, in honouring
this toast, to remember the Producers. The productions of
our West-End theatres leave a good deal to be desired, largely,
no doubt, owing to the star system, which is certainly a bad

thing, for it tends to throw the production out of scale and to unduly emphasise one part to the disadvantage of the others. We ought to discourage that as far as possible and I hope we do so successfully in this Society. I would add that it is by no means an easy thing to find good Producers. There are not many in London, and we have a grudge against the Court Theatre—perhaps our only one—in that owing to the vast amount of work he has to do there we are no longer able to get Mr. Granville Barker to produce our plays for us. His work as a producer is invaluable. With this toast I am fortunate in being able to couple the name of Miss Gertrude Kingston, for Miss Kingston is one of the most accomplished and delightful actresses we have. You are fortunate also because she is not only a delightful actress but also a delightful speaker, as many of you I am sure know already. Those of you who do not know her in the capacity of speech-maker will be glad to do so when she replies to this toast, so that I must not keep you from that pleasure any longer.

An Interview with Hankin in the Spring of 1909*

In The Days of my Youth.
My First Success.

NO. 560.—MR. ST. JOHN HANKIN.

[*Among the younger dramatists Mr. St. John Hankin occupies a distinguished position by reason of his originality of outlook and the natural logic of his treatment of his subjects. His dramatic creed is strongly and amusingly expressed in the interview which appears as this week's contribution to the "My First Success" series. In this, it will be noted, Mr. Hankin stands for the printed play which he believes ought to have a far wider vogue than it possesses, for, as he remarked to my representative, "unless a play is printed and has a chance to be read it is dead and*

*From M.A.P. 22 (10 April 1909): 348–49.

done for as soon as it no longer holds the stage. There is nothing so dead, under the present conditions, as a play which is not being acted."]

My first success! Would you not prefer that I should talk of my last failure? It would certainly be more amusing, even though it clashed with your series. You see, I do not know that I ever had a success. In the vulgar financial sense, I am sure I never have, and I do not suppose I ever shall. There is a popular delusion that the drama is a gold mine, and that all playwrights wallow in wealth. But I find no evidence for it in my own case. The "higher drama" is a very amusing game, but it's not profitable. Perhaps when the public has learned to read plays, the dramatist may be able to keep out of the Work-house, but, at present, the novelist has it all his own way, and drama is not in demand at Mudie's. That is one of my complaints against the great British public. It will buy novels, but it will not buy plays; thereby putting itself in opposition to the habit of civilised people on the Continent who read their Brieux and even their Bernstein with avidity.

THE COMMERCIAL THEATRE.

Why did I take to writing plays at all? Well, I attribute it to constitutional perversity. It seemed the most difficult line in which to succeed that presented itself. The chances of success in the London theatre of to-day for anyone save the purely commercial dramatist are infinitesimal, but in art it is only the difficult things that are worth doing, and if you are born wilful, you must either write what interests you or not write at all. So I write plays.

*　　*　　*　　*　　*　　*

My first success! How insulting of you not to know! It was called *The Two Mr. Wetherbys,* and was intended for Mr. Charles Hawtrey. Need I say he declined it? These actors never know a good thing. Various other people declined it too. Then the Stage Society produced it. It had a respectful hearing from

that decorous body, and a kindly Press assured me that it was
a meritorious little piece but only suited to a "small and cultured
audience." Since then it has toured Australia (my first success)
and won much applause in mining camps and the Backwoods
generally. It was much appreciated at Ballarat. Was I astonished?
Not in the least. All this talk about cultured audiences is the
merest bunkum. The Stage Society are the most unsophisticated
people in the world, the simplest, the most ready to be amused.
Anything which amuses them will amuse Bendigo.

AUTHOR AND ACTOR

My next play? the next was *The Return of the Prodigal.* You
never saw it, of course. Well, you missed a great pleasure. It
was played at the Court; in fact, it was the first of their series of
experimental *matinées.* It, *The Voysey Inheritance,* and *Major
Barbara*, if I remember right, made up the Autumn series.
I shall always be glad to have been No. 1 of that gallery. The
Prodigal was admirably produced and cast by Granville Barker,
and it was superbly played. A. E. Matthews, Florence Haydon,
Amy Lamborn, Dennis Eadie, how good they were! I shall
never get a better cast for a play though I live to be as old as
Pinero—which, by the way, I hope not to do. How much does
a play owe to its acting? It owes everything to its acting, just
as the actors owe everything to their author. He fiddles. They
dance. Good drama makes good actors.

You should have seen Miss Clare Greet in *The Cassilis Engagement*, and Miss Haydon in *The Charity that Began at Home.*
And all done by kindness! I have no wrangles at rehearsal to
confide to you: no awful revelations of scowls behind the scenes
and stormy passages between actor and author. I have hardly
ever come to actual blows even with Barker—which is a great
tribute to his good temper—and mine!

How did the Court people like *The Return of the Prodigal?*
I think they liked it all right. I used to go and watch them cry
in the last act. When they did that (and they generally did)

I knew it was going all right. But *The Return of the Prodigal* is a comedy? Of course it is. But that is no reason why it shouldn't make people cry. Anyhow, it does. Will there be any chance of seeing it in London in the near future? Yes, if you call Kensington London. Miss Horniman's company are playing it and *The Charity that Began at Home* at the Coronet early in June.

AN OXFORD AMBITION

Is the *Prodigal* only fitted for a "small and cultured audience"? Good heavens, no. The Court audience was just as simple and unsophisticated as the Stage Society. A child could play with them. The *Prodigal* is beloved of Manchester. It is much appreciated in Hull and draws tears from Glasgow. And it is much applauded at Oxford and Cambridge. Some day Oxford is to have a Stage Society of its own—in fact, I believe it has founded one already. In which case, I am sure, *The Return of the Prodigal* will figure in its repertory. If it does not, I shall want Gilbert Murray's head on a charger. On the whole, I do not consider the *Prodigal* an "improving" play. It is a plea for the underdog, and that is always rather immoral and subversive. "It is a very clever play, my dear," said the lady who sat behind me to her neighbour, "but I don't think we will take Johnny to it."

THE BEST PLAY

On the other hand, I think *The Charity that Began at Home* most improving. No doubt that is why it has been less popular. Mr. George Alexander tells me that I utterly spoilt it as a "business proposition" by not giving it a "happy ending." He may be right for London but it seems to do all right for the provinces, and they are reviving it shortly at Manchester, I believe. Of course, it ends happily, really. The engagement is broken off. But I won't argue that point with you. You'll find all the pros and cons in the preface to "Three plays with happy endings," which, of course, you have not read. You'd better order it at once from Boots' and get up the subject. Barker says it's the best of the plays, and I'm not sure he isn't right.

*   *   *   *   *   *

After *The Charity?—The Cassilis Engagement*. Once more the faithful Stage Society, most kindly and tolerant of audiences, so ready to be amused, so eager to laugh if you will only let them. Two dear ladies who sat behind me at the first performance of *The Two Mr. Wetherbys* murmured hoarsely that they "rather missed the deeper note," but I don't believe they minded really. And the Stage Society laughed quite good-humouredly over *The Cassilis Engagement*—who could help laughing at Mrs. Borridge when Mrs. Borridge was Miss Clare Greet, most inimitable of actresses? The Press, of course, was very cross over it. I think the London Press sometimes suffers from a kind of inverted snobbishness which made them want to sympathise with poor, vulgar, old Mrs. Borridge and her not very reputable daughter rather than with Mrs. Cassilis and "the County."

THE REVIEWER

Next in my troubled career as dramatist comes a little one-act play at the Criterion, *The Burglar Who Failed*. That was my first success! It ran seven whole weeks. Finally, *The Last of the De Mullins*. Again the Stage Society. An "uncomfortable play," they tell me. It is to be published in May—without a preface. That, at least, is good news, isn't it? Reviewers are curiously restive under prefaces. They seem to think no dramatist should have any opinion about his plays, or that, if he has, he should not express them. I suppose if you call a reviewer an ass he feels bound to resent it. He is probably so afraid it may turn out to be true.

*   *   *   *   *   *

Have I any other plays coming on in the near future? Not

so far as I know. I have a one-act masterpiece done, but I don't see who is to produce it. It wants very careful casting and it is not very well suited for the rough-and-tumble work of playing the stalls into their seats. However, we shall see about that later on. I have got a comedy—a very light comedy—struggling to come to birth, and if I only get to Algiers or somewhere where the sun shines, I may be able to write it. Nobody can possibly write a light comedy in a north-east wind, can they? A north-easter killed even Charles Kingsley.

Appendix C

Productions of Hankin's Plays with
Dates of First Performances

I. London Productions
  A. *Andrew Paterson* (written with Nora Vynne)
     Performed with *Aftermath* by Nora Vynne and *Who's
     Married* by Mrs. Adams-Acton
              Bayswater Bijou Theatre (Victoria Hall), 22
              June 1893
  B. *The Two Mr. Wetherbys*
     The Imperial Theatre (Stage Society), 15 March 1903
  C. *The Return of the Prodigal*
     Court Theatre, 26 September 1905
     Court Theatre, 29 April 1907
     Coronet Theatre, 22 May 1912 (Miss Horniman's
        Company)
     Globe Theatre, 24 November 1948
     Thorndike Theatre (Leatherhead), 23 January 1973
  D. *The Charity that Began at Home*
     Court Theatre, 23 October 1906
  E. *The Cassilis Engagement*
     The Imperial Theatre (Stage Society), 10 February 1907
     Court Theatre, 17 January 1913 (by the Merrie Andrews
        Dramatic Society, an amateur group)
     Guildhall School of Music, 22 February 1956
  F. *The Burglar Who Failed*
     Criterion Theatre, 27 October 1908
  G. *The Last of the De Mullins*
     Haymarket Theatre (Stage Society), 6 December 1908

H. *The Constant Lover*
    Performed with Galsworthy's *The Pigeon*
    Royalty Theatre, 30 January 1912
    Performed with *The New Sin* by Basil Macdonald
    Hasting
      Everyman Theatre, 7 August 1922
    Performed with Joanne Holbrook's *Lady Susan*
    New Boltons (Theatre Club), 28 March 1952
    Performed with *The Reliver* by Ray Jenkins
    Hovenden Theatre Club, 19 February 1962

I. *Thompson* (completed by George Calderon)
    Performed with Rudyard Kipling's *The Harbour
    Watch*
    New Royalty Theatre, 22 April 1913

II. Other Productions
  A. *The Two Mr. Wetherbys*
    Madison-Square Theatre, New York City, 23 August
    1906
    Royalty Theatre, Scottish Repertory Theatre, Glasgow,
    2 Nov. 1910
    Turn Verein Hall, Melbourne Repertory Theatre,
    26 June 1911
    Repertory Theatre, Birmingham, 18 September 1915
    Repertory Theatre, Liverpool, 1917–1918 season
    Little Theatre, Bristol, 9 March 1925

  B. *The Return of the Prodigal*
    Gaiety Theatre, Manchester, 11 May 1908
    Gaiety Theatre, Manchester, 15 March 1909
    Gaiety Theatre, Manchester, 19 September 1910
    Edgbaston Assembly Rooms, Pilgrim Players, Bir-
      mingham, 11 March 1911, 30 September 1911, 7
        October 1911, and 3 February 1912
    Royalty Theatre, Scottish Repertory Theatre, Glasgow,
      16 October 1911
    Repertory Theatre, Liverpool, 7 February 1912

His Majesty's Theatre, Montreal, Canada, 29 February 1912

Gaiety Theatre, Manchester, 3 March 1913

Repertory Theatre, Birmingham, 13 September 1913

Repertory Theatre, Birmingham, 16 April 1914

West Pier Theatre, Brighton production by the Birmingham Repertory Theatre Co., 16 March 1915

Theatre Royal, Leamington Spa production by Birmingham Repertory Theatre Co., 23 March 1915

Repertory Theatre, Birmingham, 15 May 1915

Repertory Theatre, Birmingham, 13 February 1920

Repertory Theatre, Birmingham, 3 February 1923

Prince's Theatre, Manchester, Birmingham Repertory production, 8 June 1923

Little Theatre, Bristol, 7 April 1924

Palace Theatre, Weston-Supermare, 11 September 1924

Royal Theatre, Brighton, 15 November 1948

Repertory Theatre, Birmingham, 21 February 1950

C. *The Charity that Began at Home*

Gaiety Theatre, Manchester, 9 November 1908

Gaiety Theatre, Manchester, 16 September 1912

Repertory Theatre, Liverpool, 24 February 1913

Repertory Theatre, Birmingham, 30 January 1915

Repertory Theatre, Birmingham, 25 March 1916

Repertory Theatre, Birmingham, 9 June 1917

The Playhouse, The Melbourne Repertory Co., 26 August 1917

D. *The Cassilis Engagement*

Royalty Theatre, Scottish Repertory Theatre, Glasgow, 4 April 1910

Royalty Theatre, Scottish Repertory Theatre, Glasgow, 30 January 1911

Gaiety Theatre, Manchester, visit by Liverpool Repertory Co., 22 March 1911

Repertory Theatre, Liverpool, 20 March and 15 April 1912

Repertory Theatre, Birmingham, 22 March 1913
Repertory Theatre, Birmingham, 24 January 1914
Grand Theatre, Woverhampton, visit by Birmingham
   Repertory Theatre, 23 February 1915
Repertory Theatre, Liverpool, 26 February 1915
Grand Theatre, Croydon, visit by Birmingham Rep-
   ertory Theatre, 2 March 1915
West Pier Theatre, Brighton, visit by Birmingham
   Repertory Theatre, 9 March 1915
Theatre Royal, Leamington Spa, visit by Birming-
   ham Repertory Theatre, 27 March 1915
Repertory Theatre, Birmingham, 22 January 1916
Repertory Theatre, Birmingham, 25 November 1916
Repertory Theatre, Birmingham, 15 September 1917
Repertory Theatre, Birmingham, 25 October 1919
Repertory Theatre, Birmingham, 1 October 1921
Repertory Theatre, Birmingham, 18 August 1923
Repertory Theatre, Birmingham, 25 January 1926
Alexandra Theatre, Birmingham, production by
   the Birmingham Jewish Arts Society, 18 December
   1928
Repertory Theatre, Birmingham, 8 March 1949

E. *The Burglar Who Failed*
   Performed with *Miles Dixon* by Gilbert Cannan and
   How He Lied to Her Husband by Bernard Shaw
      Repertory Theatre, Birmingham, 18 February 1914
   Performed with W. B. Maxwell's *The Unknown Factor*
      Repertory Theatre, Liverpool, 26 September 1921

F. *The Last of the De Mullins*
   Gaiety Theatre, Manchester, 18 August 1913
   Repertory Theatre, Birmingham, 2 March 1918

G. *The Constant Lover*
   Performed with *Ser Taldo's Bride* by Barry V. Jackson
   and John Drinkwater and *Re Pilgridge* by L. B.
   Chatwin
      Repertory Theatre, Birmingham, 14 June 1913

Performed with *His Excellency the Governor* by Robert Marshall

    Repertory Theatre, Birmingham, 6 June 1914

Performed with Frederick Fenn's and Richard Pryce's *The Love Child* and Oscar Wilde's monologue, *The Happy Prince*

    Repertory Theatre, Liverpool, 16 November 1915

Little Theatre, Bristol, 31 March 1924

Performed with *The Proposal* by Chekhov and *A Phoenix Too Frequent* by Christopher Fry

    Repertory Theatre, Birmingham, 6 September 1949

Performed with Jean-Jacques Bernard's *The Unquiet Spirit*

    Liverpool Repertory Co., 25 November 1953

Performed with Dylan Thomas's *Return Journey* and Christopher Fry's *A Phoenix Too Frequent*

    Grand Theatre, Swansea, The Welsh Theatre Co., 4 November 1969

H. *Thompson*

    Repertory Theatre, Birmingham, 17 February 1917

Selected Bibliography

In the following bibliography I have annotated those entries whose titles reveal little about their subjects; those entries for the Hankin manuscripts; and, finally, from the maze of short items that Hankin wrote for *Punch*, those entries which shed light on Hankin's other writings, particularly his plays.

To Sister de Chantal Whelan for her research in London and for her alphabetical listings of both Hankin's reviews in *The Times* and his numerous items in *Punch* (appended to her unpublished dissertation), I—and all subsequent students of Hankin—stand indebted. Parts of her two lists I have corrected, annotated, and included in this bibliography.

Works by St. John Hankin

A. Plays (including selected reprintings)

Andrew Paterson: A one-act play by Nora Vynne and St. John Hankin. *Theatre*, n. s. 22 (1 July 1893): 34–40.

The Burglar Who Failed. In *The Dramatic Works of St. John Hankin*, 1912 (below); reprinted in *The Plays Of St. John Hankin*, 1923 (below).

The Cassilis Engagement: A Comedy for Mothers. In *Three Plays with Happy Endings*. London and New York: Samuel French, [1907]; reprinted in *Representative British Dramas: Victorian and Modern*. Edited by M. J. Moses. Boston: Little, Brown, 1918, and Boston: Brown & Co., 1931; reprinted in *Contemporary Plays*. Edited by T. H. Dickinson and J. R. Crawford. Boston: Houghton Mifflin, 1925; reprinted in *Late Victorian Plays*. Edited by George Rowell. London: Oxford University Press, 1968.

The Charity that Began at Home: A Comedy for Philanthropists. London: Martin Secker, 1906; reprint. London: Martin Secker, [1914].

The Constant Lover: A Comedy of Youth in One Act. London
and New York: Samuel French, 1912; reprinted in *Theatre Arts
Magazine* (New York) 3 (1919): 67–77; reprinted in *One-Act
Plays of To-day.* Compiled by J. W. Marriott. 4th ser.
London: G. G. Harrap, 1928, pp. 261–79.

The Dramatic Works of St. John Hankin. Edited by John Drinkwater.
3 vols. London: Martin Secker, and New York: M. Kennerley,
1912. [Includes Hankin's five full-length plays,
Burglar and *Constant*, plus six of his essays—five of
them from the *Fortnightly Review.*]

The Last of the De Mullins: A Play without a Preface.
London: A. C. Fifield, 1909; reprinted in *Twentieth Century
Plays.* Edited by F. W. Chandler and R. A. Cordell. New York:
T. Nelson & Sons, 1934. 1: 97–127.

The Plays of St. John Hankin. Edited by John Drinkwater. 2 vols.
London: Martin Secker, and New York: George H. Doran,
1923. [Includes Hankin's five full-length plays,
Burglar, Constant, and *Thompson.*]

The Return of the Prodigal: A Comedy for Fathers. New York
and London: Samuel French, 1907; reprint. London: Richards
Press, 1949; reprinted in *Edwardian Plays.* Edited by Gerald Weales.
New York: Hill & Wang, 1962.

Thompson: A Comedy in Three Acts by St. John Hankin and
George Calderon. London: M. Secker, and New York: Mitchell
Kennerley, 1913; reprint. London and New York: Samuel French,
1924.

Three Plays with Happy Endings. London and New York: Samuel
French, [1907]. [Includes *Return, Charity, Cassilis,* and a "Preface."]

The Two Mr. Wetherbys: A Middle-Class Comedy. New York and
London: Samuel French, 1907; reprint. New York and London:
Samuel French, 1921.

B. Parodies, Satires, and Miscellaneous Short Pieces

1. Forty-four Short Dramatizations in *Punch*, June 1898–December 1903
(arranged chronologically)

Hamlet, 11 June 1898, pp. 268–69.

Antigone, 2 July 1898, p. 310.

Julius Ceasar, 23 July 1898, p. 25.

Macbeth, 17 September 1898, p. 121.

Five Novels

The Egoist, 18 January 1899, p. 36.

H. Rider Haggard's *Dr. Therne*, 1 February 1899, pp. 59–60.

Anthony Hope's *Phroso*, 15 March 1899, pp. 124–25.

Mrs. Hodgson Burnett's *A Lady of Quality*, 22 March 1899, pp. 136–37.

Hall Caine's *The Christian*, 25 October 1899, pp. 196–97.

Maeterlinck's *Pelléas and Mélisande*, 25 January 1899, p. 39.

H. V. Esmond's *Grierson's Way* and Freeman Wills's *The Only Way*, 1 March 1899, pp. 100–101.

Berte Thomas' and Granville Barker's *The Weather-Hen*, 19 July 1899, pp. 27–28.

C. B. Fernald's *The Moonlight Blossom*, 11 October 1899,   pp. 178–79.

George Fleming's [pseud.] *The Canary*, 6 December 1899,   pp. 274–75.

Richard Ganthony's *A Message from Mars*, 20 December 1899, pp. 299–300.

The 14 items later reprinted as *Mr. Punch's Dramatic Sequels*

The School for Scandal, 2 January 1901, pp. 14–15.

Sheridan's *The Critic*, 9 January 1901, pp. 34–35.

Hamlet, 16 January 1901, pp. 50, 52.

Much Ado about Nothing, 23 January 1901, pp. 68, 70.

Euripides's *Alcestis*, 6 February 1901, pp. 118, 120.

She Stoops to Conquer, 13 February 1901, pp. 126, 128.

Lytton's *The Lady of Lyons*, 20 February 1901, pp. 146, 148.

Robertson's *Caste*, 27 February 1901, pp. 162, 164.

Fitzgerald's *The Rubáiyát of Omar Khayyám*, 6 March 1901, pp. 180, 182.

Gilbert's *Patience, or Bunthorne's Bride*, 20 March 1901, pp. 214, 216.

A "Dramatic Prologue" to Pinero's *The Notorious Mrs. Ebbsmith*, 27 March 1901, pp. 234, 236.

Pinero's *The Second Mrs. Tanqueray*, 1 May 1901, pp. 322, 325.

Ibsen's *The Lady from the Sea*, 8 May 1901, pp. 339–40.

Shaw's *Caesar and Cleopatra*, 15 May 1901, pp. 357–58.

Macbeth, 11 September 1901, pp. 193–94, 18 September, p. 203, 25 September,

p. 221, & 2 October, p. 235.

Coriolanus, 30 October 1901, pp. 314–15 and 6 November 1901, pp. 325–26.

Clyde Fitch's *The Last of the Dandies*, 18 December 1901, pp. 438–39.

Maeterlinck's *Ardiane et Barbe Bleue*, 1 January 1902, pp. 5–6.

Six "national dramas"

In the "newest Homeric school," 5 March 1902, p. 170.

In "the modern Political *genre* of which Mr. Anthony Hope is the inventor," 12 March 1902, p. 188.

"An adaptation from the French" by Sydney Grundy, 9 April 1902, p. 258.

Kipling's *The Jungle Book*, 14 May 1902, pp. 349–50.

Paolo and Francesca, 4 June 1902, pp. 404–5.

Poet laureate Mr. Austin's poem, *A Tale of True Love*, 9 July 1902, pp. 6–7.

Four "Compressed dramas" of current British plays

H. A. Jones's *Chance, the Idol*, 22 October 1902, pp. 287–88.

J. H. McCarthy's *If I Were King*, 12 November 1902, pp. 340–41.

Hall Caine's *The Eternal City*, 26 November 1902, pp. 376–77.

Cutcliffe Hyne's *The Adventures of Captain Kettle*, 3 December 1902, pp. 384–85.

Gorki's *The Lower Depths*, 9 December 1903, pp. 403–4.

2. Other, Selected Writings in *Punch* (October 1898–January 1909)

"The Actor-Manager Explains," 6 July 1904, p. 2. [A satire on actor-managers.]

"Another 'Real Conversation,' " 19 June 1901, p. 462. [A satire at the expense of William Archer.]

"Anticipations," 23 April 1902, p. 290. ["With suitable apologies to Mr. H. G. Wells," but Hankin satirizes violent spectators at sporting matches, not Wells and his book.]

"Babs the Insufferable. An Undramatic Sequel," 26 June 1901, p. 470. [A parody of Frances Elizabeth MacFall's recent novel, *Babs, the Impossible*.]

"A Ballad of the Congo," 30 April 1902, p. 322. [Poem satirizing colonial exploitation in the Congo.]

"Clifford's Inn and After," 29 April 1903, p. 290. [Satire against destroying old buildings.]

" 'Coelum Nec Animum Mutant,' " 10 January 1900, p. 20 and 17 January

1900, p. 43. [A "Diary of one who 'can't stand winter time in England.' "]

"Comments of a Housemaid," 28 May 1902, p. 384. ["*In humble emulation of the 'Comments of a Countess,' which have recently been adorning a weekly journal.*"]

" 'Cramming' for the Army," 7 November 1900, p. 327. [Satire on army regimentation.]

"Criminal Jurisprudence à la Mode," 22 October 1898, p. 185. [A satire on applying the theory that society, and not the criminal, is responsible for crime.]

"De Gustibus—" 27 August 1902, p. 127. [Poem satirizing mountain climbing, reprinted in *Lost Masterpieces*.]

"Diary of a 'Peace' Orator," 28 March 1900, p. 220. [The diary writer speaks against the Boer War, but crowds jeer him and beat him up.]

"The Diary of a Successful General," 10 December 1898, p. 268. [Satirizes public adoration of military leaders.]

"Diary of a Would-be Member of Parliament," 29 October 1898, p. 197. [Illustrates a daily paper's observation "that in a large number of constituencies the essential qualities of a good Party candidate are neither eloquence nor knowledge, but an imperturable good temper, a thick skin, and a long purse."]

"From a Sabine Farm," 30 May 1906, p. 386. [This poem reveals country noises are louder than city noises.]

"Half-a-Dozen 'Leagues' under the Sea," 1 February 1899, p. 60. [A brief sequel to Verne's story.]

"Hamlet for Ladies," 31 May 1899, p. 256. [Describes what touches Sarah Bernhardt will bring to her playing of Hamlet.]

"Hamlet's Soliloquy (New Style)," 21 January 1903, p. 44 and 1 May 1907, p. 307. [The second entry is a satire of Beerbohm Tree, who claimed he could improvise forgotten lines.]

"A Hard Case," 13 September 1905, p. 197. [On the difficulties of writing stories.]

"Home Thoughts from at Home," 18 October 1899, p. 185. [Poem about unpleasant autumn English weather, alluding, of course, to Browning's "Home-Thoughts, from Abroad."]

"L'Homme Incompris," 17 April 1901, p. 294. [Speaker of the poem, a city clerk, expresses his disappointment with Pinero's recent confession that he could not write plays about the middle classes.]

"A Horrible Imbroglio," 5 June 1901, pp. 423–24. [Narrator of this brief story has sent a proposal of marriage via the post; his letters and his intended's do not reach each other, and, in the meantime, he has found a new romantic interest.]

"An Imaginary Conversation," 7 May 1902, p. 330. [Satirizes Oxford University's rules and administration.]

"An Interesting Papyrus," 8 October 1898, p. 161. [Satire of scholars.]

"The 'Iris' Club," 11 December 1901, p. 422. [A satire of Pinero's play.]

"Jeers, Idle Jeers!" 3 April 1901, p. 253. [Not a parody of Tennyson's "Tears, Idle Tears," but a poem about the poet's numerous (mock?) aspirations; reprinted in *Lost Masterpieces.*]

"Journalism à la Mode," 15 October 1902, p. 262. [Satire of Journalists.]

"Leaves from an Aeronaut's Diary," 16 October 1901, pp. 278-79. [On the dangers of flying.]

" 'The Lordliest Life on Earth,' " 6 January 1904, p. 14. [Poem satirizing German military discipline; reprinted in *Lost Masterpieces.*]

"The Modern Dramatist to His Muse," 6 January 1909, p. 10. [Autobiographical poem, partly about Hankin's failure, along with other serious playwrights of his time, to win a following.]

"Morituri Saluntant!" 23 July 1902, p. 52. [Poem satirizing America; reprinted in *Lost Masterpieces.*]

"Mr. Punch's Dramatic Recipes: I.—How to Write a Celtic Drama," 14 June 1899, p. 285. [A satire of Edward Martyn's *The Heather Field*, then playing in London; Hankin's piece also has a barb for William Archer.]

_____: II.—How to Write a 'Gleeful Plenitude,' " 5 July 1899, p. 1. [A satire of George H. Broadhurst's *Why Smith Left Home.*]

_____: III.—How to Write an Anglo-Indian Drama," 12 July 1899, p. 16. [A satire of H. A. Jones's *Carnac Sahib* and Gilbert Murray's *Carlyon Sahib*, both recently staged in London.]

_____: IV.—How to Be an Actor-Manager," 16 August 1899, p. 76. [A satire on the power and misjudgment of actor-managers.]

_____: V.—How to Be a Dramatic Critic," 23 August 1899, p. 88. [A satire which by implication reveals the qualities Hankin admires in a critic, including judiciousness.]

"Mr. Punch's Dreyfus Dictionary," 15 October 1898, p. 179.

"Mr. Squeers on the Emotions," 16 November 1904, p. 355. [Poem about mothers as subjects for poetry.]

"My Friend Binks," 4 February 1903, pp. 88–89. [Brief story on the pains and boredom of visits by a former classmate.]

"A New Philanthropic Society," 5 November 1898, p. 213. ["For the Rescue of Unsuccessful Professional Men" from overcrowded professions.]

"Ode to Spring/By a Gourmet," 24 May 1905, p. 370.

"On Bank Holidays," 10 April 1901, p. 272. [Prose satire on bank holidays, similar in its criticisms to Hankin's earlier article, "The Sins of St. Lubbock" (below).]

"Pooh-poohri from a Surrey Back Garden," 1 April 1903, p. 218. [Satire on gardening writing.]

"Reflections of a Motor-Racer," 10 July 1901, p. 27. [Satire on automobile racing.]

"Rhymes for the *Times*," 1 Novemberr 1899, p. 214. [Poem satirizing a Swinburne sonnet recently printed in the *Times*.]

"Rule, Britannia!" 11 November 1903, p. 332. [Satire on the dress regulations of the British navy.]

"See How They Run (Or Ought To Do)," 21 December 1904, p. 438. [Revised English nursery rhymes.]

"The Simpler Life," 15 April 1903, pp. 269–70. [Brief story about a couple's failure to achieve a "simpler life" without the help of the wife's maid.]

"The Struggle for Life; Or, 'Don't Cry Till You're Out of the Willow-wood,'" 15 February 1899, p. 77. ["A Sonnet Sequence after–some distance after– Rossetti."]

" 'The Tempest' in a Tea-cup," 9 May 1900, p. 330. [A satire on abridged productions of Shakespeare, particularly those by Beerbohm Tree.]

"The Trials of the Telephone," 17 October 1900, p. 276. [Satire on the inefficient London telephone system.]

"An Unappreciated Genius," 20 May 1903, p. 347. [Poem by caterpillar who is the cause of the nightingale's song; reprinted in *Lost Masterpieces*.]

"Urbs in Rure," 3 July 1901, p. 5. [About the difficulty of buying fresh foods in the country.]

"The Way They Have in the Army," 14 November 1900, p. 344. [Satire on the large expenditures necessary to remain a cavalry officer.]

"Where's Air?" 6 November 1901, p. 326. [Poem satirizing polluted London fog.]

3. Parodies and Satires in Book Form

Dramatic Sequels. London: Martin Secker, 1925 or 1926 & New York: Minton, Balch & Co., 1926. [Contains the 14 dramatizations of *Mr. Punch's Dramatic Sequels* minus the "Dramatic Prologue" to Pinero's *The Notorious Mrs. Ebbsmith.*]

Lost Masterpieces and Other Verses. London: A. Constable, 1904. [Contains verse parodies and light verse, nearly all of which originally appeared in either *Punch* or *St. James's Gazette.* Poets parodied include Wordsworth, Byron, Scott, Shelley, Burns, Tennyson, Browning, Rossetti, Swinburne, Arnold, and Kipling.]

Mr. Punch's Dramatic Sequels, with fourteen original illustrations by E. J. Wheeler. London: Bradbury, Agnew, [1901].

C. Reviews

1. In the *Academy* (all signed)

" 'Caesar and Cleopatra' at the Savoy." 73 (30 November 1907): 196–97.

"Court Theatre." 70 (10 February 1906): 141–42. [Reviews of Robert Vernon Harcourt's *A Question of Age* and of Frederick Fenn's *The Convict on the Hearth.*]

Review of *Li Hungchang,* by Prof. Douglas, 48 (7 September 1895): 179–80.

"Mr. Bernard Shaw's 'Discussion.' " 69 (2 December 1905): 1265–66. [A review of *Major Barbara,* which had just been produced for the first time, by the Court Theatre.]

"The New Technique." 69 (4 November 1905): 1178. [A review of Granville Barker's then new play, *The Voysey Inheritance.*]

"Realism at the Court." 72 (13 April 1907): 369–70. [Reviews of Galsworthy's *The Silver Box* and Elizabeth Robins's *Votes for Women!*]

"The Stage Society." 72 (30 March 1907): 320–21. [A review of Brieux's *Les Hannetons.*]

"The Stage Society–The 'Moscow School' of Drama." 72 (15 June 1907): 585–86. [Reviews of Charles McEvoy's *David Ballard* and Frank Wedekind's *Der Kammersänger.*]

Review of *Studies in Prose and Poetry,* by Algernon Charles Swinburne, 46 (29 December 1894): 547–48.

" 'The Weather-Hen.' " 57 (15 July 1899): 67. [A review of the play by Berte Thomas and Granville Barker.]

2. Selected Drama Reviews in the *Times,* August 1897–December 1899 (all unsigned)

Boucicault, Aubrey, and Shillingford, Osmond. *A Court Scandal*, 11 May 1899, p. 12, col. 6.

Broadhurst, George H. *The Last Chapter*, 5 September 1899, p. 8, col. 6.

_____ *Why Smith Left Home*, 3 May 1899, p. 3, col. 2.

Bulwer-Lytton, Edward. *The Lady of Lyons*, 25 August 1898, p. 5, col. 6.

_____ *Richelieu*, 14 June 1899, p. 6, col. 3.

Caine, Hall. *The Christian*, 17 October 1899, p. 6, col. 6.

Carl, Frederick. *His Majesty's Musketeers*, 10 May 1899, p. 12, col. 4. [A dramatization of Dumas's novel.]

Dumas fils, Alexandre. *La Femme de Claude*, 2 July 1898, p. 18, col. 5.

Fernald, Chester Bailey. *The Ghetto*, 11 September 1899, p. 6, col. 4. [An adaptation from Heijermans's play of the same title.]

_____ *The Moonlight Blossom*, 10 October 1899, p. 5, col. 6.

Fitzgerald, Edward. *Such Stuff as Dreams Are Made of*, 16 May 1899, p. 13, col. 5. [An adaptation from a Spanish play by Calderón.]

Fleming, George [pseud.]. *The Canary*, 16 November 1899, p. 6, col. 6.

Ganthony, Richard. *A Message from Mars*, 23 November 1899, p. 6, col. 4.

[Goldberg, M.] *The Man in the Iron Mask*, 13 March 1899, p. 8, col. 1. [Adaptation from Dumas's romance.]

Grundy, Sydney. *A Marriage of Convenience*, 6 September 1897, p. 5, col. 2. [An adaptation.]

Harte, Bret, and Pemberton, T. Edgar. *Sue*, 30 June 1898, p. 10, col. 2. [An adaptation of one of Harte's stories.]

Jones, Henry A. *The Liars*, 25 July 1898, p. 3, col. 5. [A revival.]

Jones, Henry A., and Herman, Henry. *The Silver King*, 4 September 1899, p. 10, col. 4. [A revival.]

Jonson, Ben. *The Alchemist*, 25 February 1899, p. 14, col. 4.

Kálidàsa. *Sakuntalà*, 4 July 1899, p. 12, col. 3.

Pinero, A. W. *Sweet Lavender*, 23 February 1899, p. 6, col. 4. [A revival.]

Robertson, Thomas W. *Caste*, 20 March 1899, p. 3, col. 3. [A revival.]

_____ *David Garrick*, 26 July 1898, p. 8, col. 3.

Ross, Adrian, and Carr, O. (Music). *In Town*, 10 August 1897, p. 4, col. 6. [A burlesque.]

Rostand, Edmond. *Cyrano de Bergerac*, 5 July 1898, p. 6, cols. 3–4; 28 June 1899, p. 4, col. 5.

Scribe, Augustin, and Legouve, Ernest. *Adrienne Lecouvreur*, 28 June 1898, p. 7, col. 6.

Scribe, Augustin; Legouve, Ernest; and Halevy, L. (Music). *The Jewess*, 29 June 1899, p. 4, col. 2.

Shakespeare, William. *As You Like It*, 22 June 1899, p. 8, col. 4.

——— *King Richard the Third*, 12 September 1899, p. 8, col. 6.

——— *A Midsummer Night's Dream*, 9 February 1899, p. 10, col. 2.

——— *Othello*, 23 August 1898, p. 4, col. 3; 8 February 1899, p. 10, col. 6.

Shaw, Bernard. *The Devil's Disciple*, 27 September 1899, p. 8, col. 6.

Sophocles. *Antigone*, 21 June 1898, p. 11, col. 6.

Swinburne, Algernon Charles. *Locrine*, 21 March 1899, p. 13, col. 5.

Thomas, Berte W. and Barker, Granville. *The Weather-Hen,* 10 July 1899, p. 14, col. 4.

Wilde, Oscar. *A Woman of No Importance* 2 December 1899, p. 5, col. 6. [A revival.]

Wills, Freeman. *The Only Way*, 20 February 1899, p. 13, col. 3. [An adaptation of Dickens's *A Tale of Two Cities*.]

3. In *The Times Literary Supplement* (unsigned review)

"Some Minor Verse" 10 July 1903, p. 217. [Reviews of *The Lonely Way* by W. A. Adams, *Love Songs and Little Lyrics* by J. A. Middleton, *Verses Occasionally Humorous* by E. H. Lacon Watson, and *Horace on the Links* by C. J. B. and P. S. W.]

D. Essays

"The Censorship of Plays," *Academy* 74 (29 February 1908): 514–15.

"The Collected Plays of Oscar Wilde." *Fortnightly Review*, n.s. 83 or o.s. 89 (1 May 1908): 791–802; reprinted in *Dramatic Works*, 3: 181–201.

"The Criminal." *Westminister Review* 140 (July 1893): 24–30; reprinted in *Eclectic Magazine of Foreign Literature, Science, and Art* (N.Y.) 124 (April 1895): 478–82.

"The Disturbance on the Niger." *Times* (London), 2 March 1895, p. 16, col. 4. [This short article is unsigned, but the Editorial Diaries in the Archives of the *Times* reveal Hankin to be its author.]

"How to Run an Art Theatre for London." *Fortnightly Review*, n.s. 82 or o.s. 88 (1 November 1907): 814–18; reprinted in *Dramatic Works*, 3: 171–79.

"The Making of a Masterpiece." ["Sundry Short Stories and Essays."] London, n.d. [One of five pieces in the author's hand; in portfolio at the University of Illinois Library, Urbana. On the first page the manuscript is signed "St. John E C [*sic*] Hankin/11 Addison Road/Bedford Park." In this ten-page essay Hankin argues that great poems result from being filtered through the generations by word of mouth. He cites as examples the ballads, the poems of Homer, and the work of the classical poets and prose writers and of Shakespeare. He also argues that printing freezes inappropriate words and phrases into poems.]

"Mr. Bernard Shaw as Critic." *Fortnightly Review*, n.s. 81 or o.s. 87 (1 June 1907): 1057–68; reprinted in *Dramatic Works*, 3: 149–70.

"The Need for an Endowed Theatre in London." *Fortnightly Review*, n.s. 84 or o.s. 90 (1 December 1908): 1038–47; reprinted in *Dramatic Works*, 3: 203–21.

"Nonsense Verses, New and Old." *Idler* 14 (August 1898): 90–98.

"Old Friends with a New Face." *Fortnightly Review* 68 (August 1897): 297–303. [On the spelling of Indian words.]

Preface to *Three Plays with Happy Endings*. London: Samuel French, [1907]; reprinted as "A Note on Happy Endings." In *Dramatic Works*, 3: 119–29.

"The Propagandist as Playwright" ["Sundry Short Stories and Essays."] London, n.d. [One of five pieces in the author's hand; in portfolio at the University of Illinois Library, Urbana. The first page of the manuscript is signed "St. John Hankin/62 Gower St. W.C." From internal evidence it is possible to date this essay as early 1904. In this fourteen-page essay Hankin argues that great drama has an ethical intention; some dramatists keep it from obtruding more skillfully than do other playwrights. He then examines the drama of Brieux, who, he says, is usually a moralist first, a playwright second. At some length Hankin shows how Brieux's *Les Trois Filles de M. Dupont* treats serious social problems in an uncompromising yet dramatic and compelling manner. He concludes that the English theater needs such serious yet commercial drama, and he hopes Bernard Shaw may yet provide it.]

"Puritanism and the English Stage." *Fortnightly Review*, n.s. 80 or o.s. 86 (1 December 1906): 1055–64; reprinted in *Dramatic Works*, 3: 131–48.

"Shakespeare for Amateurs." *Academy* 53 (5 March 1898): 264–65.

"The Sins of St. Lubbock." *Nineteenth Century* 41 (March 1897): 467–73. [An essay on British bank holidays.]

"[Robert Louis] Stevenson as Humorist." *Academy* 53 (18 June 1898): 667–68.

"A Study in Fog." ["Sundry Short Stories and Essays."] London, n.d. [One of five pieces in the author's hand; in portfolio at the University of Illinois Library, Urbana. On the first page of the manuscript Hankin has written: "St. John E C [*sic*] Hankin/11 Addison Road/Bedford Park." A four-page description of a foggy beach off the Isle of Wight in the early morning. The piece is similar in subject matter to Hankin's essay "The True Sublime of Boating."]

"The True Sublime of Boating." *Longman's Magazine 31,* (February 1898): 359–66; reprinted in *Eclectic Magazine of Foreign Literature, Science, and Art* (N.Y.) 130 (April 1898): 520–24.

E. Fiction

"The Counsel of Myronides." *Belgravia* 82 (October 1893): 193–203. [Set in ancient Greece, the story focuses on the individualistic philosophy and action of General Myronides.]

"The Course of True Love–." Chiswick, n.d. [Typescript of an apparently unpublished novel; in the University of Illinois Library, Urbana. Title page has original title "A Question of Expediency" crossed out. Also on the title page are typed and deleted Hankin's initials "E. C." and two addresses: 11 Addison Road/Bedford Park/Chiswick and 62 Gower St./W.C. These deletions suggest that Hankin wrote the story sometime in the 1890s, then took the manuscript with him to his residence on Gower Street, where he lived from approximately 1901 to 1905, then finally took it to his retirement in Campden, Gloucestershire. The 120-page manuscript tells how an idealistic young woman is outraged when she learns of her new husband's old affair but is eventually won over by her relatives, who argue for an acceptance of the world even if it is often not as one might wish it.]

"The Lodge-Keeper at Market-Ashton." ["Sundry Short Stories and Essays."] London, n.d. [One of five pieces in the author's hand; in portfolio at the University of Illinois Library, Urbana. The first page is signed "St. John E. C. Hankin/11 Addison Road/Bedford Park." The seven-page short story tells of the impecunious Sir John Ffolliott's arranging a marriage for his aged, widower lodge-keeper, in order that there will be someone around to do the work.]

"A Man of Impulse." *English Review* 2 (June 1909): 485–99; reprinted in *Living Age* 262 (3 July 1909): 36–46. [The story suggests that charity is ineffectual for a man ill-equipped to survive and that he is better off drowning himself.]

"The Philosopher's Ghost." ["Sundry Short Stories and Essays."] London, n.d. [One of five pieces in the author's hand; in portfolio at the University of Illinois Library, Urbana. The story is unsigned and is incomplete and cannot be dated from internal evidence. In this five-page fragment a philosopher returns home one evening, finds what claims to be the ghost of a philosopher, and they talk.]

F. Translations

The Three Daughters of M. Dupont. In *Three Plays by Brieux . . . with Preface by Bernard Shaw.* New York: Brentano's, 1911 & 1914.

G. Letters (arranged chronologically)

To William Blackwood & Son, Publishers. The National Library of Scotland. Ms. nos. 4551 (1890); 4572 (1891); and 4587 (1892). [The letters enclosed with three mss Hankin submitted for publication: "Sleep Mr. Speaker," a parody of Praed's poem, "Up Mr. Speaker" (1890); "The Gentleman Ranker," a short story (1891); and the ms "Father and Son" (1892).]

"The Vacant Laureateship." *Times* (London), 3 January 1895, p. 4, col. 3.

"Some Remarks on *Julius Caesar.*" *Academy* 53 (5 February 1898): 160–61.

"More Remarks on *Julius Caesar.*" *Academy* 53 (5 March 1898): 269.

"*Macbeth* at the Lyceum." *Academy* 54 (1 October 1898): 335–36.

"The Threatened Destruction of Clifford's-Inn." *Times* (London), 21 April 1903, p. 8, col. 5.

Times (London), 28 April 1903, p. 15, cols. 1–2. [Another letter about the destruction of Clifford's-Inn.]

"Motor-Cars in the Park." *Times* (London), 3 July 1903, p. 15, col. 1. [Hankin criticizes the noises and smells of cars in Hyde Park.]

"The District Railway." *Times* (London), 19 January 1906, p. 12, col. 2.

To H. G. Wells. Rare Books Room, University of Illinois Library, Urbana. [Letter is dated August 16, but the internal evidence is unmistakable that Hankin meant October 16, 1906. In this brief letter Hankin offers Wells a complimentary ticket to one of Hankin's plays; Hankin also praises Galsworthy's *The Silver Box* and urges Wells to see it.]

"The Smoke Nuisance." *Times* (London), 20 November 1906, p. 16, cols. 5–6.

To H. G. Wells. Rare Books Room, the University of Illinois Library, Urbana. [Dated December 3. The internal evidence is strong that this letter is also from 1906. In it, Hankin praises Wells's recent book, *The Future in America* (published in 1906). Hankin, though, says he doesn't think any "ism," including socialism, can save the world, given man's nature. Nonetheless, Hankin thinks Wells's book brilliant and particularly praises Wells for exposing the American reception of Maxim Gorki. (After the press learned that Gorki was travelling with his mistress, it attacked him unmercifully; thereafter hotels refused him rooms. In the uproar the injustices in Russia which Gorki had come to proclaim were forgotten.)]

"*Antony and Cleopatra.*" *Times* (London), 30 January 1907, p. 12, col. 2.

To H. G. Wells. Rare Books Room, University of Illinois Library, Urbana. [Dated February 13. From the internal evidence, the year must be 1907. Wells had just seen a performance of Hankin's *The Cassilis Engagement* and written Hankin about it, evidently with a note of criticism about Mrs. Cassilis' handling of her son's imprudent engagement. Hankin humorously defends that approach to handling the problem, then thanks Wells for seeing the play and for writing.]

"The Society of Authors." *Times* (London), 29 March 1907, p. 6, col. 2.

"The Lord Chamberlain and *The Mikado.*" *Times* (London), 6 May 1907, p. 11, cols. 5-6 & 9 May 1907, p. 3, col. 3.

"The Need for a National Theatre." *Times* (London), 23 March 1908, p. 3, col. 6.

To Mrs. Wheeler. Rare Books Room, University of Illinois Library, Urbana. [Dated May 13. This four-page letter is written to the actress who played Violet in the May, 1908, production of *Return* in Manchester. Hankin suggests that Mrs. Wheeler discontinue all stage business while she gives Violet's impassioned speech late in the play. Hankin concludes that he is admittedly tiresome, but that he is happy that the first performance was a success.]

"'Temperance' Again." *Times* (London), 25 November 1908, p. 8, col. 3. [On the sale of methylated spirit on Sundays.]

"Cet Animal Est Très Méchant." *Nation* 4 (19 December 1908): 472. [Hankin's criticism of William Archer's review of *The Last of the De Mullins.*]

"Mr. Archer and *The Last of the De Mullins.*" *Nation* 4 (16 January 1909): 611-12.

"The Abolition of Capital Punishment." *Times* (London), 16 January 1909, p. 8, col. 3.

To G. Herbert Thring. Manuscript Room, The British Library. Add. Ms. No. 57002. [Dated February 28. The placement of the letter within the file suggests that the note is from 1909. In it Hankin merely asks Thring if Hankin might talk with him briefly.]

"Drama Censorship," *Times* (London), 2 June 1909, p. 13, col. 3.

H. Interviews

"In the Days of my Youth." *M.A.P.* [*Mainly About People*] 22 (10 April 1909): 348–49. [Reprinted in Appendix B.]

I. Speeches

Stage Society News, no. 20 (24 March 1906), pp. 73–74. [Reprinted in Appendix B.]

Works about St. John Hankin

A. Bibliographic Entries

Batho, Edith C., and Dobrée, Bonamy. Bibliography. *The Victorians and After, 1830–1914*. 3d ed. London: Cresset Press, 1962, pp. 257–58.

Clark, Barrett H. *The British and American Drama of To-Day*. N.Y.: Henry Holt, 1915, pp. 108–9; enlarged and reprinted in *A Study of the Modern Drama*. New York: D. Appleton, 1925, pp. 292–93.

Engel, Gertrud. *St. John Hankin als Dramatiker*. Ph.D. dissertation, Giessen, 1931. Giessen: Buchdruckerei Nitschkowski, 1931, pp. 4–6 (below).

Lauterbach, Edward S., and Davis, W. Eugene. "Hankin." *The Transitional Age: British Literature 1880–1920*. Troy, N.Y.: Whitston Publishing Co., 1973, p. 167.

"St. John Emile Clavering Hankin." *The New Cambridge Bibliography of English Literature*. Edited by I. R. Willison. Vol. 4. Cambridge: The University Press, 1972, pp. 950–51.

B. Biographical Sources

1. Biographical Reference Works

"Hankin, St. John." *Who Was Who: A Companion to "Who's Who" Containing the Biographies of Those Who Died During the Period 1897–1916*. London: A & C Black, 1920. 1: 312.

W[oods], G[abriel] S. "Hankin, St. John Emile Clavering." *The Dictionary of National Biography, Supplement 1901–1911*. Edited by Sir Sidney Lee. Oxford University Press, 1912, p. 196.

2. Obituaries, Funeral Notice, Will Notice

Daily Chronicle, 21 June 1909, p. 5, cols. 1–4.

Daily Graphic, 21 June 1909, p. 12, cols. 1–3.

Daily News, 21 June 1909, p. 7, col. 4.

Englishman (Calcutta), 12 July 1909, p. 6, cols. 4–5.

Era, 72 (26 June 1909): 10, cols. 1–2.

Evesham Standard and West Midland Observer, 26 June 1909, p. 6, col. 2.

Oxford Review, 21 June 1909, p. 4, col. 1. [The Oxford and Cambridge undergraduate journals were incorporated with this paper.]

Radnor Express, 24 June 1909, p. 3, cols. 1–2.

Radnorshire Standard, 26 June 1909, p. 10, col. 1.

Times (London), 21 June 1909, p. 10, cols. 4–5.

———— 22 June 1909, p. 13, col. 4.

———— 23 June 1909, p. 13, col. 1.

———— 5 Aug. 1909, p. 9, col. 4.

3. Articles about Hankin Occasioned by His Death

Beerbohm, Max. "A Note on St. John Hankin." *Saturday Review* 107 (26 June 1909): 810; reprinted in *Last Theatres 1904–1910*. London: Rupert Hart-Davis, 1970, pp. 473–74.

"Mr. St. John Hankin." *Athenaeum*, no. 4261 (26 June 1909), p. 768.

"The Theatres." *Truth* 65 (23 June 1909): 1507–8.

4. Other Sources, Mainly Biographical

Bennett, Arnold. "St. John Hankin." *Books and Persons*. London: Chatto & Windus, 1917, pp. 140–42.

———— "Friday, January 24th. [1908]." *The Journals of Arnold Bennett: 1896–1910*. Edited by Newman Flower. London: Cassell & Co., 1932, pp. 276–77.

Pinero, Arthur W. "234. To G. B. Shaw." *The Collected Letters of Sir Arthur Pinero*. Edited by J. P. Wearing. Minneapolis: University of Minnesota Press, 1974, pp. 226–27.

Shaw, Bernard. "To Alfred Sutro," "To Arthur W. Pinero." *Collected Letters*

1898–1910. Edited by Dan H. Laurence. New York: Dodd, Mead, 1972, pp. 847–50, 911–13.

C. Books

Engel, Gertrud. *St. John Hankin als Dramatiker.* Ph.D. dissertation, University of Giessen, 1931. Giessen: Buchdruckerei Nitschkowski, 1931.

D. Dissertations

Hirsch, Foster Lance. "The Edwardian Drama of Ideas." Ph.D. dissertation, Columbia University, 1971. [Includes a seventy-five-page chapter on Hankin's drama.]

O'Neill, John Drew. "The Comedy of St. John Hankin." Ph.D. dissertation, University of Michigan, 1954.

Phillips, William H. "St. John Hankin and the Drama of the Stage Society and the Court Theatre." Ph.D. dissertation, Indiana University, 1972.

Stein, Rita Louise. "The Serious Comedy of St. John Hankin and Harley Granville [*sic*] Barker: A Study of Two Edwardian Contemporaries of Shaw." Ph.D. dissertation, Columbia University, 1972. [Includes a 100-page essay on Hankin's drama.]

Whelan, Sister Mary de Chantal. "St. John Hankin's Dramatic Esthetic: Its Theory and Practice." Ph.D. dissertation, Indiana University, 1973.

E. Sections in Books

Agate, James E. "Mr. Drinkwater and St. John Hankin." *The Contemporary Theatre, 1923.* London: Leonard Parsons, 1924, pp. 24–27.

_____ "Hankin." *A Short View of the English Stage 1900–1926.* London: Herbert Jenkins, 1926, pp. 87–95.

Cunliffe, John W. "St. John Hankin (1860 [*sic*]–1909)." *Modern English Playwrights.* 1st ed., 1927; reprint. Port Washington, N.Y.: Kennikat Press, 1969, pp. 122–29.

Downer, Alan S. "The Court Playwrights." *The British Drama.* New York: Appleton-Century-Crofts, 1950, pp. 311, 312, 317–18.

Drinkwater, John. "St. John Emile Clavering Hankin, Playwright, 1870 [*sic*]–1909." *Forum* 48 (12 December 1912): 713–29; slightly enlarged and reprinted as Introduction to *Dramatic Works,* 1: 3–28; reprint. "St. John Hankin." *Prose Papers.* London: Elkin Mathews, 1918, pp. 224–60; reprint. Introduction to *The Plays of St. John Hankin,* 1: 3–24.

Ervine, St. John. Introduction to *The Return of the Prodigal,* by St. John Hankin. London: Richards Press, 1949, pp. 5–14.

Howe, P. P. "St. John Hankin and His Comedy of Recognition." *Fortnightly Review* 99 (January 1913): 165–75; reprinted in *North American Review* 197 (January 1913): 78–89; reprinted in "St. John Hankin." *Dramatic Portraits,* 1st ed., 1913; reprint. Port Washington, N.Y.: Kennikat Press, 1969, pp. 163–83.

MacCarthy, Desmond. *The Court Theatre 1904–1907.* 1st ed., 1907; reprint. Edited by Stanley Weintraub. Coral Gables: Univ. of Miami Press, 1966.

Morgan, A[rthur] E[ustace]. "Hankin." *Tendencies of Modern English Drama.* New York: Charles Scribner's Sons, 1924, pp. 111–120.

Nicoll, Allardyce. "The Play of Ideas: Harley Granville-Barker, St [*sic*] John Hankin and John Galsworthy." *English Drama 1900–1930.* Cambridge: The University Press, 1973, pp. 396–99.

———. "St [*sic*] John Hankin and Others." *British Drama.* 4th ed. London: George G. Harrap, 1947, pp. 379–82.

Phillips, William H. "St. John Hankin." *The Reader's Encyclopedia of English Literature.* Edited by Edgar Johnson. New York: Thomas Y. Crowell, in press.

F. Periodical Articles

Curle, Richard. "St. John Hankin's Plays." *Bookman* (London) 46 (July 1914): 172.

Evans, T. F. "A Note on Hankin." *Shavian* 4 (Winter 1969–70): 52–53.

Menon, K. P. Karunakara. "St. John Hankin." *Journal of the Annamalai University* 8 (March 1939): 131–45.

Meyerstein, E. H. W. "St. John Hankin." *English* 7 (Spring 1949): 175–79.

Moses, Montrose J. "The Advance-Guard of British Dramatists." *Metropolitan Magazine* (N.Y.) 37 (December 1912): 31, 32, 53, 54.

Nethercot, Arthur H. "The Quintessence of Idealism; or, The Slaves of Duty." *PMLA* 62 (1947): 844–59.

Phillips, William H. "The Individual and Society in the Plays of St. John Hankin." *Shavian* 4 (Spring, 1972): 170–74.

———. "An Unexpected Delight." *Non Solus:* A Publication of the University of Illinois Library Friends, no. 1 (1974), p. 34. [A notice about the manuscript of Hankin's novel, "The Course of True Love–."]

"St. John Hankin and the 'New Movement.' " *American Playwright* 3 (June 1914): 207–13.

Sowers, William Leigh. "The Plays of St. John Hankin." *Texas Review* 3 (October 1917–July 1918): 117–32.

Storer, Edward. "Dramatists of To-day VI–." *British Review* 5 (January 1914): 80–87; reprinted in *Living Age* 280 (January–March 1914): 781–84.

Tucker, Marion. "The Plays of St. John Hankin." *Theatre Arts Magazine* 3 (1919): 78–80.

G. Book Reviews (arranged chronologically)

1. *Mr. Punch's Dramatic Sequels*
   Academy 61 (30 November 1901): 503–4.

2. *Lost Masterpieces and Other Verses*
   Academy 67 (15 October 1904): 336–37.
   Athenaeum no. 4016 (15 October 1904): pp. 515–16.
   Spectator 93 (22 October 1904): 599–600.

3. *Three Plays with Happy Endings*
   Academy 73 (28 September 1907): 941–42.
   Athenaeum, no. 4189 (8 February 1908), p. 172.
   Nation (London) 2 (9 November 1907): 194.
   Nation (New York) 85 (26 September 1907): 288.
   Times Literary Supplement, 13 September 1907, p. 278.

4. *The Last of the De Mullins*
   Athenaeum, no. 4270 (28 August 1909), p. 248.
   Nation (New York) 88 (27 May 1909): 543.
   Times Literary Supplement, 7 October 1909, pp. 357–58.

5. *The Constant Lover*
   Revue Germanique 8 (May–June 1912): 304–5. [In French.]

6. *The Dramatic Works of St. John Hankin*
   Athenaeum, no. 4442 (14 December 1912): p. 739.
   Boston Evening Transcript, 20 March 1913, p. 14, cols. 5–6. [Part of this review is reprinted from *Times Literary Supplement* of 9 January 1913.]
   Dial 55 (1 December 1913): 474–76. [By Archibald Henderson.]
   Nation (London) 12 (28 December 1912): 580.
   Nation (New York) 96 (27 March 1913): 315.
   New York Times 18 (13 April 1913): 220. [By John Palmer.]
   Saturday Review 114 (21 December 1912): 776.
   Spectator, Supplement 110 (25 January 1913): 131.
   Times Literary Supplement, 9 January 1913, p. 13.

7. *Thompson*
   Bookman (Completed by George Calderon) (London) 44 (September 1913): 268–69.
   Times Literary Supplement, 15 May 1913, p. 205.

8. *The Plays of St. John Hankin*
   Nation & The Athenaeum 33 (25 August 1923): 665–66. [By Raymond Mortimer.]
   New Statesman 21 (21 July 1923): 450–51.
   Saturday Review 136 (14 July 1923): 47–48.
   Times Literary Supplement, 28 June 1923, pp. 429–30.

9. *Dramatic Sequels*
   The Saturday Review 141 (10 April 1926): 480.

H. Selected Dramatic Reviews (arranged chronologically)

1. *Andrew Paterson* (Co-authored with Nora Vynne)
   Era 55 (24 June 1893): 10, col. 1.
   Referee, no. 828 (25 June 1893), p. 3, col. 2.
   Stage, no. 641 (29 June 1893), p. 11, cols. 3–4.
   Dramatic Review 16 (1 July 1893): 6–7.

2. *The Burglar Who Failed*
   Daily Chronicle, 28 October 1908, p. 7, col. 3.
   Daily Mail, 28 October 1908, p. 5, col. 6.
   Times (London), 28 October 1908, p. 15, col 4.
   Era 72 (31 October 1908): 17, col. 4.
   Graphic: 78 (31 October 1908): 530.
   Sketch 64 (4 November 1908): 110.
   Truth 64 (4 November 1908): 1073.

3. *The Cassilis Engagement*
   Daily Chronicle, 12 February 1907, p. 3, col. 6.
   Daily Mail, 12 February 1907, p. 5, col. 6.
   Pall Mall Gazette, 12 February 1907, p. 3, col. 2.
   Times Literary Supplement, 15 February 1907, p. 54. [By A. B. Walkley.]
   Academy 72 (16 February 1907): 169.
   Athenaeum, no. 4138 (16 February 1907), p. 207.
   Era 70 (16 February 1907): 15, col. 2.
   Saturday Review 103 (16 February 1907): 199–200. [By Max Beerbohm; reprinted in *Last Theatres 1904–1910.* London: Rupert Hart-Davis, 1970, pp. 276–79.]
   Sketch 57 (20 February 1907): 172.
   Truth 61 (20 February 1907): 450–51.
   Glasgow Herald, 5 April 1910, p. 9, col. 6.
   Glasgow Herald, 31 January 1911, p. 9, col. 2.
   Manchester Guardian, 23 March 1911, p. 7, col. 5.
   Evening Express (Liverpool), 16 April 1912, p. 7, col. 4.

Argus (Melbourne), 16 September 1912, p. 15.
Era 76 (25 January 1913): 17, col. 1.
Birmingham Daily Mail, 24 March 1913, p. 4, col. 4.
Birmingham Daily Mail 27 January 1914, p. 7, col. 5.
Birmingham Post, 17 September 1917, p. 2, col. 7.
Birmingham Post, 19 December 1928, p. 11, col. 5.
Times, 23 February 1956, p. 5, col. 2.

4. *The Charity that Began at Home*
   Daily Chronicle, 24 October 1906, p. 5, col. 5.
   Daily Mail, 24 October 1906, p. 5, col. 4.
   Pall Mall Gazette, 24 October 1906, p. 2, col. 3.
   Times Literary Supplement, 26 October 1906, p. 361. [By A. B. Walkley.]
   Academy 71 (27 October 1906): 422–23.
   Era 70 (27 October 1906): 17, col. 2.
   Graphic 74 (27 October 1906): 546.
   Saturday Review 102 (27 October 1906): 512. [By Arthur A. Baumann.]
   Sketch 56 (31 October 1906): 78.
   Truth 60 (31 October 1906): 1046.
   Manchester Guardian, 10 November 1908, p. 7, col. 6.
   Evening Express (Liverpool), 25 February 1913, p. 6, col. 6.
   Birmingham Daily Mail, 1 February 1915, p. 5, col. 5
   Argus (Melbourne), 27 August 1917, p. 3.

5. *The Constant Lover*
   Pall Mall Gazette, 31 January 1912, p. 5, col. 3.
   Era 75 (3 February 1912): 17, col. 2.
   Sketch 77 (7 February 1912): 142.
   Birmingham Daily Mail, 16 June 1913, p. 4, col. 5.
   Era 85 (9 August 1922): 4, col. 5.
   Times, 29 March 1952, p. 9, col. 5.

6. *The Last of the De Mullins*
   Daily Mail, 8 December 1908, p. 4, col. 2.
   Pall Mall Gazette, 8 December 1908, p. 10, col. 2.
   Truth 64 (9 December 1908): 1383.
   Times Literary Supplement, 10 December 1908, p. 463. [By A. B. Walkley.]
   Era 72 (12 December 1908): 19, col. 4.
   Graphic 78 (12 December 1908): 738.
   Nation 4 (12 December 1908): 431–32. [By Wm. Archer.] [This review triggered letters by Hankin (19 December), "An Old Playgoer" (2 January 1909), Archer (9 January), then Hankin again (16 January).]
   Saturday Review 106 (12 December 1908): 726–27. [By Max Beerbohm; reprinted in *Last Theatres 1904–1910.* London: Rupert Hart-Davis, 1970, pp. 413–15.]

Sketch 64 (16 December 1908): 302.
Black & White 36 (19 December 1908): 832, col. 3.
Manchester Guardian, 19 August 1913, p. 9, col. 2.
Birmingham Daily Mail, 4 March 1918, p. 5, col. 6.

7. *The Return of the Prodigal*

Daily Chronicle, 27 September 1905, p. 6, col. 6.
Daily Mail, 27 September 1905, p. 3, col. 4.
Pall Mall Gazette, 27 September 1905, p. 4, col. 2.
Times Literary Supplement, 29 September 1905, p. 316. [By A. B. Walkley.]
Academy 69 (30 September 1905): 1010.
Athenaeum no. 4066 (30 September 1905), p. 444.
Era 69 (30 September 1905): 15, col. 1.
Graphic 72 (30 September 1905): 411.
Sketch 51 (4 October 1905): 452.
Black & White 30 (7 October 1905): 482.
Saturday Review 100 (7 October 1905): 463–64. [By Max Beerbohm; reprinted in *Around Theatres.* New York: Alfred Knopf, 1930, pp. 506–510; reprint. London: Rupert Hart-Davis, 1953, pp. 392–96.]
Daily Chronicle, 30 April 1907, p. 6, col. 2.
Times, 30 April 1907, p. 5, col. 6.
Academy 72 (4 May 1907): 442–43.
Era 70 (4 May 1907): 18, col. 1.
Illustrated London News 130 (4 May 1907): 670.
Manchester Guardian, 12 May 1908, p. 7, col. 6.
Manchester Guardian, 16 March 1909, p. 7, col. 5.
Manchester Guardian, 20 September 1910, p. 7, col. 4.
Glasgow Herald, 17 October 1911, p. 7, col. 4.
Evening Express (Liverpool), 8 February 1912, p. 6, col. 5.
Times, 23 May 1912, p. 12, col. 3.
Argus (Melbourne), 2 October 1912, p. 6.
Manchester Courier, 4 March 1913, p. 8. col. 5.
Birmingham Gazette, 15 September 1913, p. 4, col. 7.
Times, 25 November 1948, p. 7, col. 4 and p. 10, col. 5. [Latter citation is for a photograph of John Gielgud and Dame Sybil Thorndike from the 1948 London production.]
Theatre Arts Magazine 33 (April 1949): 36. [By Eric Bentley. On page 33 is a large photograph from the production.]
Theatre World 45 (January 1949): 6–7. [Page 7 has three photographs from the production.]
Guardian (London edition) 25 January 1973, p. 12, cols. 3–4.
Times, 25 January 1973, p. 19, cols. 7–8.
Sunday Telegraph, 28 January 1973, p. 18, cols. 1–2.

8. *Thompson* (Completed after Hankin's death by George Calderon)
   Daily Chronicle, 23 April 1913, p. 7, col. 2.
   Daily Mail, 23 April 1913, p. 5, col. 4.
   Pall Mall Gazette, 23 April 1913, p. 7, cols. 3-4.
   Times, 23 April 1913, p. 10, col. 4.
   Academy 84 (26 April 1913): 531-32.
   Era 76 (26 April 1913): 14, col. 4.
   Illustrated London News 142 (26 April 1913): 548.
   Saturday Review 115 (26 April 1913): 517-18. [By John Palmer.]
   Sketch 82 (30 April 1913): 102.
   Truth 73 (30 April 1913): 1108-1109.
   Birmingham Daily Mail, 19 February 1917, p. 5, col. 5.

9. *The Two Mr. Wetherbys*
   Dramatic Criticism. Vol. 5. London: Eveleigh Nash, 1905, pp. 45-47.
      [By J. T. Grein. Review is dated 16 March 1903.]
   Daily Chronicle, 17 March 1903, p. 8, col. 7.
   Pall Mall Gazette, 17 March 1903, p. 10, col. 1.
   St. James's Gazette, 17 March 1903, p. 18, col. 2.
   Truth 53 (19 March 1903): 737.
   Times Literary Supplement, 20 March 1903, pp. 89-90. [By A. B. Walkley.]
   Academy 64 (21 March 1903): 282-83.
   Athenaeum no. 3934 (21 March 1903), p. 379.
   Era 66 (21 March 1903): 15, col. 5.
   Graphic 67 (21 March 1903): 394.
   Illustrated London News 122 (21 March 1903): 420.
   Saturday Review 95 (21 March 1903): 356-57. [By Max Beerbohm; reprinted in *More Theatres 1898-1903.* New York: Taplinger, 1969, pp. 546-50.]
   Sketch 41 (25 March 1903): 362.
   Black & White 25 (28 March 1903): 430-31.
   New York Times, 24 August 1906, p. 7, col. 1.
   Era 70 (15 September 1906): 18, col. 1. [A review of the New York production.]
   Glasgow Herald, 3 November 1910, p. 7, col. 5.
   Argus (Melbourne), 27 June 1911, p. 6.
   Age (Melbourne), 27 June 1911, p. 7.
   Australasian (Melbourne), 1 July 1911, p. 41.
   Argus (Melbourne), 4 July 1911, p. 9.
   Punch (Melbourne), 6 July 1911, p. 35.
   Argus (Melbourne), 8 October 1913, p. 10.
   Birmingham Daily Mail, 20 September 1915, p. 5, col. 2.

Index